Get it Done Faster!
Secrets of Dissertation Success

Moonswept Press, Inc.
20203 Goshen Road #374
Gaithersburg, MD 20879

www.CompleteYourDissertation.com

ISBN: 978-0-9718629-1-3

To Deepak
Whose love and support remain
constant, shining, and true.
I am blessed to have you in my life.

How Doing Your Dissertation is Like Eating an Ice Cream Cone

Think back, a moment, to the last ice cream cone you had. Maybe it was a double dip chocolate chip with sprinkles (my favorite!) or simple vanilla. In any case, I would like you to take a moment and think about how you approached eating that ice cream cone.

Did you take a big, deep bite out of it?

How was it to try and swallow that solid lump of cold ice cream? The last time I tried this, I got "brain freeze", a headache and my teeth hurt. It was not enjoyable.

Contrast this to a time where you might have eaten the ice cream leisurely, taking small bites and licks, slowly and patiently wearing it down. You were, perhaps, lost in the moment, yet focused on the outcome.

How is this related to the dissertation?

Many times, graduate students approach the dissertation from perspective number 1- they try to bite off huge pieces and cram their way through it- ending up with "brain freeze", headaches, stress, and an unpleasant feeling about the whole thing.

Students who approach the dissertation from the second perspective take longer to wear down the ice cream. They have to be patient, keep track of the melting and dripping, but most of all, they have to have faith that they will, indeed, get to the bottom of the scoop.

Break down the dissertation, one small bite at a time, and you, too, will get to the bottom of the scoop!

Table of Contents

Get it Done Faster!

Why do you want this degree?

Congratulations! The mere fact you're reading this book suggests that you have completed many years of schooling and are now contemplating the completion of your dissertation so that you may obtain your Ph.D.

You probably didn't get to this point without hearing some stories-probably some good and some bad-about the dissertation process. Unfortunately, the bad stories seem to carry much more weight. Many graduate students come to this phase of their education feeling uncertain and confused about what it takes to really complete their dissertation in a timely fashion.

In my work as a dissertation coach and as editor of The All But Dissertation Survival Guide, I've worked with hundreds of graduate students directly and thousands indirectly. Through this work, I have had the opportunity to better understand what qualities are necessary for a successful dissertation process. In fact, with the support and structure of the coaching framework, many of my former clients completed their dissertations in a year or less, even those who had been ABD for more than twelve years when we began working together. The process doesn't need to drag on to be meaningful; you can complete the project within a year and get on with your life.

Through this book, it is my intention that you will find

11

many strategies to propel you into completing your dissertation as quickly and as easily as possible. One of the main questions to ask yourself as you begin or proceed on your dissertation journey is "Why do I want this degree?" Now, this may seem like a very basic question and might be simple to answer, but I'm going to ask you to consider it anyway. More than anything, the dissertation process is a measure of your own perseverance and diligence in reaching your goal. It is not a test of skill or native intelligence. If you remember why you are pursuing this goal in the first place, you can use this understanding as a strong initial motivator for making progress. My request is that you take a few minutes to think about why you are pursuing this degree.

Questions to Consider:
•What led you to this field?
•What do enjoy most about your areas of study?
•How did you pick your topic?
•Why is this topic the best one to pursue right now?
•What are some fears you're having about the dissertation process?
•What will you do to combat them?
•Do you believe you'll be successful in this project?
•What are your unique talents that will help you succeed?

Before you move on in this book, I'll ask you to take some time and consider these questions very deeply. They will help you uncover your own level of desire and motivation for this degree. If you take the time to write down your answers down, perhaps in a dissertation journal or notebook, you will find your responses to be a source of comfort in the times of stress, anxiety, confusion, and worry that accompany various phases of the dissertation process.

Some truths about the process

As we move ahead, I'd like to discuss with you several truths about the dissertation process. These truths are not scientifically documented, but are strongly supported anecdotally.

Truth number one: You are smart enough.

There are times during the process that you'll feel over-whelmed and uncertain. "Am I smart enough?" "Can I do this?" "Do I have what it takes?"

These worries and doubts are quite common and will like-ly stay with you for a while. That doesn't mean that you should listen to them or doubt your own abilities.

You may wonder if you're smart enough to learn all you need to know. You are.
You may wonder if you'll be able to finish this long jour-ney. You will.
You may wonder if you have what it takes. You do.

The dissertation process is, more than anything, a test of your perseverance and focus. It is not, and has never been, a test of your own intelligence (except, perhaps, when you wonder if you were nuts to even start the Ph.D. in the first place!) You have already proven on numerous occasions that you are smart enough and capable enough.

Even when the process stalls out or the project doesn't proceed as planned, you are still capable of getting this done. No matter how difficult the journey, there is a way to reach the destination.

You have what it takes to complete this project. If you didn't, you wouldn't have come this far. If you were not able to do this, the academic gatekeepers would have stopped you long ago. And, besides, if you really, really knew you couldn't do it-if the outcome was 100 percent certain-you probably wouldn't even be trying. The uncertainty and doubt means that you kind of know-but aren't sure-and this is a good place to be. It might not be easy, but you can do this.

You are smart enough and capable enough. You can do this.

Truth number two: You are not an imposter.

Many of my former dissertation coaching clients describe that they suffer from "Imposter Syndrome." For those of you who don't know this term, it refers to someone who is "playing a role" and therefore believes that his/her success is due to "tricking" others. People with Imposter Syndrome can live in mortal dread of being found out or "uncovered." What this most often means, in my experience, is that there is a huge gap between the person's accomplishments and his/her own self view.

For example, do you know someone who is really wonderful, but who just can't see it? Or who has achieved amazing success, but believes it could be taken away at any second? Or, that s/he wouldn't have achieved it in the first place if s/he hadn't fooled everyone along the way?

Do you ever feel this way yourself?

I think we all must feel a bit of Imposter Syndrome every now and then. We sometimes fake that we know what we're doing, and we sometimes step out into a bigger game or a bigger world before we're quite ready. The key, I think, is knowing that you can grow into the bigger shoes or bigger game or bigger space.

And, of course, the second step is in accepting that you have every right to be there- because you are, indeed, who you say you are. You have every right to get your Ph.D. There are so many people who have accomplished this already; why can't you be one of them?

Truth number three: It's not about intelligence.

Let me make it clear right here that the Ph.D. is not a measure of your intelligence. It is not a secret IQ test that will somehow determine that you are not smart enough or are an imposter. Completing the dissertation has always been and will always be more about your abilities to independently organize, research, and write on a particular topic. In essence, and you probably have heard this before, the dissertation is like a series of related term papers.

The simplicity of this idea is often lost on graduate students who believe that the dissertation is supposed to be the summation of their life's work. Actually, the dissertation is more of a practical exam, like a driver's test. Presumably, once your degree is complete, you will have at least ten or more years of work ahead of you. Rather than looking at the dissertation as a summation of your life's work to date, could you see it as a practical exam, which predicates your movement into your true work? By keeping the dissertation in its proper perspective, you will find it easier to recognize that the dissertation is the "exam" you must pass before moving on.

Where so many graduate students tend to get derailed is in thinking that their dissertation is somehow correlated to the level of success they've had so far and is a predictor of how much success they will experience in the future. Again allow me to remind you that the dissertation is only a very long term paper. By now, you've written hundreds of them. You can do this one too.

The main factor that separates a Ph.D. from an ABD is that the Ph.D. has persevered in completing the final term paper. Ph.D.s understand that the dissertation is not a measure of how smart they are but an instrument to demonstrate their ability to think critically and to transfer their thoughts to paper. It's nothing more and nothing less.

Truth number four: The process is simple, but not easy.

So often, graduate students believe that the dissertation process is overwhelmingly difficult or should be extremely easy. The truth is that the process is simple; as I've said, the dissertation is just a long term paper. Conceptually, it should be simple to jot down some ideas, and it should be simple to research them. If you can keep your dissertation process this simple and, some would say, this cut-and-dried, you are very likely to move through it with a minimum of difficulty or strain. However, most graduate students tend to think of the dissertation as a process that is much more complex and difficult. Self-fulfilling prophecies suggest that we get what we think about. If a graduate student begins the dissertation process fearing its complexity and difficulty, that is very likely what s/he will experience.

Often, our own negative thoughts and beliefs about the demands of the dissertation process make the project more difficult. If you can remember that the dissertation is meant to be a relatively simple process of critical thinking, organizing, writing, and refining, you'll be far ahead of many other graduate students. In addition, if you can remember that the process is a clear one, even when it doesn't feel that easy, you'll be even further ahead.

A dissertation is easy to write once you have all the information gathered, the organization defined, and the ability to produce on paper all the ideas you've been considering. To get to this point, you must pass through some difficult terrain. There will be times where you must delay gratification as you work through your ideas, there will be times where you need to say no to fun activities, and there will be times where you struggle with feeling like you have come to the end of all you know-and you're still in chapter 1. During those times, if you can remember that the process is simple but might not always be easy, you'll create within yourself the perseverance, patience, and diligence that are crucial for dissertation success.

Truth number five: The dissertation is very doable, even when it seems otherwise.

When I work with my clients, individually and in groups, I help them create a plan for finishing the dissertation in a year or less. When I started coaching, many graduate students were surprised and amazed that I believed that a process as important and esteemed as the dissertation could be (or should be) completed in such a relatively short amount of time.

While I agree that certain kinds of dissertations are not amenable to this one-year format (for example, studies that take a longitudinal view, require enormous amounts of data, or involve long-term naturalistic observation), it has been my experience that the majority of dissertations can be researched and written within a year. My clients have proven this to be true on numerous occasions.

The unfortunate part is that very often, ABDs let the dissertation fall to the wayside and never explore how doable the project really is. It is my belief that people who have completed all of the necessary prerequisites for the dissertation really do desire the Ph.D.

However, very often, life seems to step in and derail the ABD's progress. It is my experience that the longer one is ABD, the greater the likelihood that there will be negative life experiences that serve to maintain the ABD status. So, by extension, my belief is that the quicker you can get in, through, and out of the ABD process, the better. The ideas presented in this book will help you do just that.

One of the most important aspects of this truth is that you must believe you can attain your desired outcome. The moment that you start doubting whether obtaining your Ph.D. is possible, you set into motion a whole cascade of negative thoughts, feelings, and evidences to support your doubt. Instead, I would encourage you to strengthen the belief that the dissertation is just another process to complete, and that you too can do it.

In a process of this length with so many elements of uncertainty, it is natural that you will at times doubt your abilities and capacities. When this happens, I would encourage you to contact other Ph.D.s and use this interaction as a reminder that if they did it, so can you.

More than anything, it is your belief in your own abilities that will see you through the challenges of the dissertation.

Qualities that will help you get through

In my work, I found that there are several qualities that separate the successful ABD from the less successful one. Again, while my information is not scientifically based, there is a great deal of anecdotal evidence to support the validity of my assertions.

Clarity

In the first section of the book, I asked you to take a few minutes to clarify why you are pursuing this degree. I hope you took the time to get clear on that. If you didn't or if you want to spend more time getting clear, I would encourage you again to think about your long-term vision, goals, and desires. If you don't have clarity on these areas, you won't know where you're going. If you don't know where you're going, you'll never know when you get there.

Why did you decide to pursue your Ph.D. in the first place? What are other academic goals you've successfully attained? How will your Ph.D. make a difference to the world? Who will be served by your teaching, research, and other academic skills?

When you can answer these questions fully and align them with your core values and your strengths, you will shift the dissertation from a "have to" that is externally imposed to a "want to" that is internally driven.

In most cases, you will have sacrificed a lot to get to this stage of academic achievement. What are the benefits to you and others that can be found in your completing your degree?

As you think about this, don't worry about sounding grandiose or conceited. In many cases, there will be some reason why you chose this particular career path. Revisiting your reasons, thinking, and approach can provide a strong internal foundation and some structure for rising to the challenges of the dissertation process.

When you think of happy people that you know--friends, colleagues, neighbors, or co-workers-have you ever stopped to consider what secret these people have found in order to live happily?

While in many cases living happily can come from opti-mism-the sense of hope and possibility for the magic of life-not all happy people are optimists. Happy people don't always believe that every cloud has a silver lining or that the glass is always half full. Instead, the quality that I believe separates happy people from those who are less happy is that happy people have found a way to create their lives in accordance with their values. Happy people are clear on what's important, and take action to bring more of what they value into their everyday lives.

Most dissertators are not that happy. Here's why: they haven't found a way-yet-to express their true values in the pursuit of their degree. Let's say that your three core values are happiness, family, and achievement. If you are working on a section of the dissertation that you really don't like, and it's keeping you from your family, and you're not mak-ing progress ... can you see how your life is not in align-ment with your values?

Now, in contrast, let's say that you were working on your

dissertation and had made a commitment to express your values in this process. You might then find a way to make the process more joyful/happier (maybe writing outside in the sun or taking short breaks to smell the flowers), you might ask your spouse or child to assist you in some way, and you might pledge to stay focused on achieving something-no matter how small-before wrapping up for the day. Can you see the difference in the second approach? Who is likely to be happier in the process?

Aside from creating happiness, core values provide a sense of stability and freedom in terms of making important decisions. You can use your core values to decide what choices to make in your daily life. One of my core values is happiness. Each time I'm faced with a choice, I ask, "Which option would make me happiest?" Then, I use the answer as a guide to making my decision. What's been really interesting to notice is that since I began approaching things this way, my decisions are easier to make, feel better, and have had wonderfully positive outcomes! My clients also have found this method to be very effective, especially in cases where there is a lot of gray area, where both options have pros and cons. By refocusing their decision from "yes" or "no" or "right" or "wrong" to "what would make me _____ (insert one of your three core values here) ?," it is easier to make important decisions from a place of greater personal integrity and awareness.

Take some time now to think about your core values and decide how you can take steps to orient your dissertation process around your values. With some practice, you'll find that stress and worry begin to diminish, and you'll be feeling happier-and be making progress.

Positive Belief in Yourself

Another quality of successful dissertators is a reasonable sense of positivity and positive belief in their own abilities. It doesn't mean that every graduate student expects to be a

21

shining star in every aspect of the dissertation process. Instead, it means that graduate students have some internal foundation or belief that supports them in feeling good about who they are and what they can do.

Generally speaking, the climate of academia is not one that necessarily reinforces graduate students' sense of their own abilities. In some cases, graduate students are lucky enough to have mentors or advisers who promote and develop the students' own sense of their strengths. More often, unfortunately, graduate students have become so accustomed to focusing on their deficits that they find it difficult if not impossible to believe in their strengths.

If you have any doubt about your own abilities to complete this project, this will hamper you in your path. While some doubt is in all of us, we each must do whatever we can to further promote a strong sense of our own capacities.

If we think of the dissertation process as an exam that requires the blending of all the skills we've learned so far, and if we've had reasonable success up to this point, it's a natural conclusion to practice positive thinking about ourselves and our capabilities.

Though it might feel like the rules have changed completely and totally in your dissertation process-and they have, in some ways-there is still enough similarity between this process and others you've successfully completed that you can understand that you have what it takes to complete this project, too.

Good Relational Skills

High emotional intelligence-the capacity to relate well and comfortably with people-is another facet of dissertation success. My clients who were comfortable interacting with their advisers, departments, peers, and consultants in an appropriate and confident manner found it much easier to complete the dissertation in a timely fashion.

Good relational skills refers to having strong communication skills, a more direct communication style, and a presence that suggests you are in charge of your own project and how it proceeds. You are comfortable setting clear boundaries with those with whom you work and, perhaps even more crucially, are comfortable enforcing or adhering to these boundaries when necessary.

Setting and keeping boundaries can be daunting work; almost everyone feels uncomfortable doing it. However, there are ways to set and maintain boundaries appropriately with your peers, advisers (yes, even them!), and other people who have some impact on your dissertation process.

Being at ease talking with people and sharing ideas with them is another trait that can make the dissertation process easier to complete. It may be that sometimes you can't share your thoughts with those in your program (due to envy, competitiveness, or other factors). In these cases, it's important to find a group of people with whom you can share your work since, for at least a year, the dissertation will consume most of your time and efforts.

Another element to good relational skills involves being comfortable in asking for help. There are no extra points for doing the dissertation in isolation. You do need to work independently, but there is no reason you can't get help along the way. Research assistants, statistics consultants, editors, a coach, and a writing group all require that you be open to asking for help before help is provided. Too many graduate students take the hard way and waste their time, efforts, and energy on tasks that someone else could do for them, tasks that are not central to the independent thinking, critical analysis, and, yes, writing that are the hallmarks of the dissertation.

Finally, another important element of relational skills is resilience, the ability to bounce back when situations don't proceed as planned. The greater the resilience someone possesses, the faster s/he will bounce back from negative feedback, perceived rejection, or perceived failure. Low resilience seems to impede progress most significantly in the writing phase, especially when the graduate student is confronted with criticism from his/her adviser and/or dissertation writing group.

The positive news about each of these traits is that they can be strengthened before and during the dissertation process. We'll discuss more about how to build these skills in later chapters, but the benefits of improving in each of these areas will have long-lasting positive impact on your life, even after the dissertation is a fading memory.

Self Talk

One of the biggest challenges in maintaining the necessary dedication and determination to complete the dissertation can be found in an individual's self talk. Self talk, as used here, refers to the conversations that go on inside our heads.

Self talk is an important area to examine because what we think about is what we are likely to create. Self talk, unfortunately, is often very negative. Our internal voice focuses incessantly on the ways in which we're not smart enough, good enough, or capable enough. In the process as involved and lengthy as the dissertation, self talk can be a strong predictor of eventual success or failure.

How can you tell whether your self talk is positive or negative? It's actually very easy. First, you can listen to what you actually say. You'll find that if your self talk is negative, the content of what you say to yourself is filled with phrases such as "should have," "would have," and "could have." Also, you'll find that your focus seems to shift quickly from the past to the future, and that you find it very difficult if not impossible to be right here, right now. Negative self talk also makes us feel negative emotions such as stress, anxiety, worry, tension, fear, and overwhelmed. If you frequently feel exhausted, off-balance, tired, and drained, especially after you just spent a lot of time alone, it's highly probable that your self talk is primarily negative.

The very nature of the dissertation process is a solitary one. You will, before this is over, spend countless hours organizing, researching, and writing about your ideas. You will spend a lot of time thinking, refining, and polishing your ideas. Most of you will be working in a great deal of solitude and possibly isolation. If you are prone to negative thinking anyway, this tendency, left unchecked, is likely to get worse in the quiet spaces of the dissertation process. Therefore, it is important to learn how to identify and control your negative thoughts early on so that you can increase the probability that you will be successful in obtaining your goal.

In the next section, we'll talk more about ways to control your negative thinking. It is important to recognize that overcoming negative thinking through thought management is an ongoing process. It is not something that you just do once, and the "cure" sticks forever. Instead, you must commit to regular, frequent processes to manage your negative thoughts and keep them from destroying any chance of succeeding in the dissertation process.

Also, there are likely to be times when your self talk becomes more negative than usual. This may happen if you have just received criticism about your writing. Your self talk is also likely to become more negative if you are experiencing any kind of stress in your "non-dissertation" life, such as illness, relationship strain, moving to a new house, giving birth to a child, etc.

Remember, self talk is something we all do. Most of us have

very negative self talk. You must find ways to combat the negative self talk, and apply them regularly.

Self Care

An important component for diminishing negative self talk and for increasing dissertation success is the concept of self care. Self care, simply stated, is any activity you undertake for the purpose of resting, refreshing, relaxing, or rejuvenating.

Now, you may have read that last sentence and be thinking, "What is she talking about? Doesn't she know I have a dissertation to write? Doesn't she know that there is no time to rest or relax?"

I do know that you have a dissertation to write, and I know that you will accomplish the task more quickly and joyfully and meaningfully if you take care of yourself along the way. While the "basics"-eating well, sleeping well, and exercising-are all necessary foundational elements to good self care, the kind of self care I'm supporting here are activities beyond those required for life maintenance and general good health. I'm referring to more expansive, enriching, fulfilling activities, ones in which you participate and feel all your senses coming alive, activities filled with laughter, friends, and an inner sense of peace, confidence, and joy.

This is a tough sell to many graduate students, mostly, I think, because we have all become overly accustomed to delayed gratification due to all of our years in school. We are quite comfortable with planning for "someday" and much less likely to act now. Countless graduate students have said that they are "afraid that if I make time to feel good, I'll never get back to the dissertation." Is this you?

If so, that means your dissertation process is severely fun deprived. You probably are feeling stressed, overwhelmed, and anxious; you are having trouble meeting deadlines; and you might find yourself procrastinating and spinning your wheels. It's my experience that once self care is taken care of, ABDs return to the dissertation process more capable and more content with the level of dedication and commitment the process requires.

Students who refuse to make time for regular, scheduled breaks and who postpone joy are more likely to experience diminished motivation and decreasing productivity. Left unchecked, this decrease in productivity can shift quickly into procrastination, resulting in a dissertation process that takes years longer than necessary.

Hopefully, you are suitably convinced of the importance of self care. Now it's time to assess how your self care is, using this unscientific, but still useful, quiz:

1) When was the last time you felt really good?

2) Who was the last person you hugged or kissed? How long ago was this?

3) When was the last time you laughed loud and long?

4) When was the last time you felt positive about your dissertation process?

5) Do you make time to engage regularly in non-dissertation activities?

6) If so, how many of these are not related to your other responsibilities? (What percentage of time do you spend just having fun?)

Were you surprised at your answers? Most people are. It's easy, in the ongoing pressure and activity of the dissertation, to forget to take the time to rest and recuperate.

Self care, like positive thinking, is an ongoing quest. You can't just "do" self care one day and think it will hold you for the rest of the year. Instead, consider utilizing self care activities as a kind of reward for manageable goals that you've met, whether your goals were related to writing, research, or anything else.

Here are some other thoughts related to self care and how you can make it more of a priority during the dissertation process.

Self Care Potpourri

*Start by looking over all of your responsibilities aside from completing your dissertation. Figure out which items can wait, which ones you can delegate, which ones you can let go of, and which ones you can hire out. This process will allow you to keep track of where you-and you alone-really need to be spending time and effort.

For example, if you find that much of your time is going into house and child care, perhaps you can ask for more help with these areas, hire temporary help, or swap chores/activities with other people to free up some time. Keep in mind that mental strain and constant worry can be more expensive than you think, so it might make sense to consider hiring out or trading for services where possible.

Now, make a list of twenty-five items or experiences you really enjoy. Ideas might include a day at the beach, one guilt-free serving of your favorite dessert, going to a matinee movie, or an extra hour with your spouse or a best friend.

Set small goals for each week, and pair these with one or

two rewards from the list you generated above. Even if you occasionally don't meet your goals, strive to engage in at least one item from your list each week. You'll feel a lot better.

Example: After meeting a week's worth of smaller goals, allow yourself a day of relaxation. Even if you don't always meet your weekly goals, allow yourself to have fun and be happy as often as you can.

• Schedule in blocks of time for rest and relaxation. This is especially important to keep your vitality high and lower your feelings of isolation. Remember that your dissertation is only one part of your life, even though it might sometimes feel like more.

• Don't talk about your dissertation in every conversation you have. Doing this is very likely to make you feel anxious and guilty because there is always something more to be done, and you're talking about it rather than doing it. Give your worry a break.

*If anyone outside of your committee or program asks about your dissertation, always say it's going great. This will help decrease the number of questions and will help your attitude, too. You might even be motivated to make this statement a reality.

• If you find that talking about the dissertation with people in your program is helpful, then do it, as support and commiseration can be great. However, sometimes these conversations can create feelings of insecurity or unhappiness, so monitor them carefully.

• When you take a day off, make it truly "off." Don't do bits and pieces of your dissertation work here and there because you probably won't be that productive, and you won't feel relaxed when the day is over.

• Remember that your dissertation is a choice. That sounds simple, but sometimes remembering this can be very powerful. It might allow you to move from feeling overwhelmed and helpless to recognizing your capacity to make this choice and follow through on it. There is nothing worse than feeling forced to do something, so try to change that feeling if you can.

• Remember that at any time, you can choose something else. This applies to deciding not to do the dissertation and to the idea that you can choose how you feel about something. In psychology, this fits in with the technique of "reframe" in which you find another point of view on the same situation. In my practice, we call this "The Third Option," which allows us to consider various choices for the same problem. It's great for increasing creativity, too.

• Be as open as is comfortable about your feelings of stress, fear, and being overwhelmed. Express these feelings-in your journal or to your coach or other support system-and get them out of your way.

• Don't deprive yourself. A friend of mine went through the initial phases of the dissertation process and set all these weird limits on herself, like "I won't get my hair cut until I finish the first draft." Keep in mind that she was nowhere close to writing that draft, and her hair annoyed her constantly. It was the main feature of our conversations, aside from the dissertation. This sounds really silly, but it highlights how we can deprive ourselves for no reason. The length of my friend's hair had nothing to do with completion of her dissertation, aside from the fact that she was living with a pointless daily annoyance. She was wasting energy and intellect over something unrelated, and depriving herself of something that would have made her feel good. You'll be glad to know that she finally "got it" and had her hair cut at the next possible opportunity. :)

• Don't jam-pack your schedule with "musts," "shoulds," or

"have to's." Leave time for "whatever." Too often, we fill our lives and schedules with too many activities or respon-sibilities and find ourselves rushing from one "have to" to the next. You'll find that your life runs more smoothly when you can leave room for the unexpected-things that run over, run late, or otherwise don't happen as planned.

• Ask for help when you need it. A friend, family member, or coach can be a great source of support and help. Don't be afraid to reach out for help; more often than not, you'll actually get it. There is no extra credit for going through this process alone.

• Consider using a daily affirmation. This will remind you to slow down, live in the present moment, and convince your subconscious to get on board and work with you to meet your goals. When creating an affirmation, it is impor-tant to make it as clear and as short as possible, and to use the present tense.

An example would be "I meet my goals with ease," not "I wish I could meet my goals with ease." One to try: "Today, I think with clarity, write with ease, and accomplish with-out strain."

• Start to let go of the need to be perfect. Stated another way, sometimes good enough is good enough. This tip refers to the idea that we spend a lot of time worrying over many unnecessary things. Keep in mind that you're always doing the best you can, whether or not you recognize it.

• Make your work space as effective and comfortable as you can. Make your office or workroom as attractive and pleasing as possible. There is nothing worse than trying to complete a major project in too little space or without the right tools. At minimum, your work space should include a large surface for writing, note-taking, and your computer. Have a comfortable and supportive chair. Your space should be well lit, temperate, and well organized. Keep all necessary information or supplies at close reach. Ideally, your work space should be out of the way of other people to cut down on interruptions or distractions. Get in the habit of screening your calls or just letting them go directly to the answering machine or voice mail. Try to limit the amount of time you waste in checking e-mail or surfing the Internet. Make use of soothing colors, textures, sounds, or smells to keep you contented and happy as you work.

• Learn to work according to your natural rhythms and the flow of your life. First, you need to recognize those times of the day when you feel most alert and mentally clear. Try to schedule your dissertation time into these periods. Use your peak times to your advantage. One client kept insisting on working on her dissertation late at night after everyone else was asleep without considering the fact that she started to wind down and get sleepy at about 10 p.m. When we switched her to waking up a bit earlier and using the quiet time in the morning before everyone else woke up, she was able to be more effective and make more progress. Figure out what works for you.

• Learn to say no. Practice often. This tip is helpful both in the dissertation process and in life. Too often we take on new responsibilities or activities at times when we really should be saying no so that we can safeguard our time, health, and other resources. Sometimes we have to say no to others so we can say yes to ourselves.

• Get yourself into a healthful and comfortable routine, and stick with it. Though it's never too late to make positive changes, it will be good if you can practice a healthy and comfortable routine before starting the dissertation and keep it going throughout the process. This might include eating well, sleeping well, committing to regular physical activity and relaxation, and so on. It takes about twenty-one days for something to become a habit so the sooner you start, the better.

• Learn to value consistent effort rather than the quality of output. In our fast-paced and frantic world, it's very easy to become caught up in the outcome or the goal rather than the process leading up to that goal. Learn to value all your effort, no matter how small it seems.

• Use technology, as appropriate, to assist you. One of the greatest things I ever discovered was voice recognition software. This is a type of computer program that allows you to speak out loud and watch as your words are typed on the screen. Although I type fairly quickly, I found this to be very helpful on those days when I was tired or when I wanted to hear how my sentences would sound. Now, this type of software is fairly inexpensive and fairly accurate (after some training), so it might be a good option for those of you who could use some help with typing. You can train this program to recognize technical language, so it might be useful even for those of you writing in highly scientific or technical fields. Some other ideas about technology have to do with making your life easier or motivating you. When I was writing my dissertation, a friend used to send me motivational cards via e-mail, which would pop up on my computer screen and cheer me up. I also used e-mail to communicate with my friends, as this allowed us to connect without pulling us away from our work. It also made it easier to cross time zones.

• As much as possible, don't get bogged down in the negative emotions-worry, shame, guilt. They are called "negative" because they don't do anything for you.

• Remember to take periodic breaks from the dissertation process. Like anything else, this can quickly become routine and boring. Give yourself a break every now and then. You will come back refreshed, and maybe with greater insight.

• Use "dead time"-time spent waiting in airports, in lines, etc.-to highlight articles or make notations. This will increase your efficiency, and it's amazing what you can accomplish in just a small block of concerted effort.

•If you're having trouble setting goals, ask someone to set them for you. You'll immediately know if what is suggested is doable for you. Go with your instinct.

•Eat well, sleep well, and play well. Self-explanatory. Deceptively simple. Incredibly powerful.

•Laugh every day. Scientific studies show that laughing relieves stress and strengthens your immune system. Consider taping your favorite shows or renting your favorite comedies. This is even better if done with a friend or two.

•If you feel stuck or in a rut, do one thing differently for a week. This could be as small as changing your breakfast cereal or something bigger like modifying a habit. Whatever it is, the point is that is should help create some change, and that may move you out of feeling stuck. I firmly believe in the domino effect-one small shift can have big impact down the line.

•Use the talents and resources of all your friends and family. Allow them to help you. Writing a dissertation can be lonely and isolating not only for the ABD, but also for his/her family and friends who often want to help, but don't know what to do. Let your family and friends do nice things for you (you can reciprocate later) and allow everyone to support you in their own way.

One woman I coached had a great network of friends and associates who helped her with physical chores, networking, and some of the mundane bits of research. They thought it was fun to help her, and her life was a lot easier because of their help. She was able to return the favor at a later date, when two of her friends returned to school for their Ph.Ds.

• Remember that your dissertation is a means to an end, not the end itself. Whenever you feel stuck or frustrated about your dissertation, it might be helpful to remind yourself why you're doing this in the first place. Think about what your post-dissertation life will be like, and this may help you move through the frustration.

• Be gentle with yourself. You're the only you you've got.

Now, before you go on reading, please take a few minutes and schedule in some self -care-right now.

The nicer you are to yourself, the better the dissertation process will feel-and the better it feels, the easier it will be to commit to. The easier it is to commit to, the faster you will finish.

Pain? No gain

Closely tied to the concept of self care is the concept of finding the easy way. Now, as I have mentioned, there seems to be a common belief among graduate students that the more difficult the work, the more meaningful or useful or valuable it is.

The dissertation process causes many graduate students to stumble because they cannot muscle through this process by sheer force of will. Many of my former clients tell stories of completing their master's theses or other final papers in two or three days of feverish writing. They come into the dissertation process anticipating that they can behave the same way with positive results. This doesn't work. Sprinting to the finish line on a master's thesis or other long paper is possible because, usually, the criteria are different for this level of work. At the master's level, you are expected to demonstrate mastery of a particular body of knowledge. At the doctoral level, you are expected to first master existing information and then you're expected to create new knowledge. This crucial difference is what separates the wind sprint of the master's thesis from the marathon of the doctoral dissertation.

Another topic to consider at this time is the fact that the dissertation is a very interdependent process, in a way that perhaps no previous work of yours has been. The dissertation depends on the input of many different people, the inflow of different types of data, and the completion of diverse steps in a linear fashion (you can't collect data before designing your methodology, for example), so progress can very often rise or fall based on a whole host of factors that may not be immediately apparent. Your own personal emotions can have a strong impact on the dissertation as well. If you are feeling angry, tired, or overwhelmed, this will directly influence your ability to make the steady kind of progress that is vital to succeeding in this project. If there is disruption within any step of the process, it will negatively impact the entire process. So, it's important to stay aware of how you're feeling in the process and making a point of checking in regularly with yourself and other key participants.

One idea that is foreign to most graduate students is that of "taking the easy way." We are taught early on that hard work is better than easy work. We believe that the dissertation should be a difficult process and, sometimes, we make it even more difficult than it needs to be by choosing overly complex topics, purposely obscure or unwieldy study design, and difficult analyses. From the beginning of the process when you are considering topics, through your qualifying/comprehensive exams, and straight up through to your dissertation process, I want to encourage you to find the easiest way to accomplish your goals. Easy can still be meaningful. And the definition of "easy" will depend on your own particular talents, your dissertation topic, and the other demands of your life. However, by orienting yourself to the question, "What will be easy and meaningful?" early on, you will short-cut some of the common pitfalls of dissertation delay. By emphasizing quality output and an easy process, your subconscious mind will present you with simple, elegant solutions and other information to smooth your way. This might sound strange, but if you'll try it, you'll find, as my clients have, that this works. By continually orienting yourself to the easiest ways to accomplish your goals, you'll achieve greater success much more easily.

If you're ready to start looking for the easy way, you can try the following: Consider what part of the dissertation process you are most fearful of. Now, quickly, brainstorm thirty ways to make the process easier. If you like, you can use a creative thinking technique called the A-Z list. In this list, you write down the letter A and a solution that begins with the letter A. Then you write the letter B and a solution that begins with the letter B, and so on. If you do this quickly and with focus, you will generate a large number of viable solutions to help you address your fears. This is a useful technique anytime you want to increase your range of thinking on a particular topic. Let's take an example-recruiting participants for your study.

A: Ask people to tell their friends
B: Buy a list of qualified names
C: Call 150 people from the phone book
D: Drop off fliers around town.
E: Envelopes-do a direct mailing
F: Friends-ask my friends how they recruited
G: God-pray that I will get enough subjects
H: Help-ask for help

... and so on. Like with any brainstorming/creative technique, you want to make sure that you don't censor your ideas prematurely. The point of this exercise is to get you thinking in new ways. Then, after generating the list, you will skim back over it and find two to three items that you want to pursue. Remember, the more you focus on completing this project in an easy and meaningful way, the more often you will take actions that support this focus.

One final thought about this topic-that you don't get extra points for suffering. Your dissertation is not inherently more praiseworthy because you suffered through it. Yes, I agree that there is some personal growth that happens through this process, and that, sometimes, can be difficult. However, the tendency to make it more difficult than necessary, the tendency to deny yourself pleasure or happiness in the process, and the tendency to unnecessarily prolong the process because you need to prove your intelligence or worth all fall under the heading of needless suffering. Needless suffering can never bring you anything valuable. You don't need to prove your worth to anybody, nor do you need to suffer for your art. You will have enough time later in your career to be competitive, critical, and long-suffering if you choose to do so. In this period, though, when so much is dependent on you finishing the process, you will want to keep your competitiveness, criticism, and suffering to a minimum. Stay away from all situations that leave you feeling bad, and do what you can to avoid creating these for yourself.

Preparing your life for the dissertation guest

When I coach clients who are just starting out in the dissertation process, we describe the time spent preparing to start working as "inviting the dissertation guest." Similar to having a houseguest for the weekend, there is often a certain amount of pre-event preparation you need to complete before you can invite the guest (or the dissertation) fully into your life. You might, for example, need to clear out space in which to work, or you might need to wrap up some remaining schoolwork or other projects before you can establish the pattern and process of working on the dissertation.

As you begin the dissertation process, you may notice that you feel a certain amount of uncertainty and anxiety. This is completely understandable, as you will be moving from the structure and regimen of graduate school and comprehensive exams to the more open-ended work of the dissertation. Certainly, you will need to become more comfortable in setting your own deadlines and in developing your own capacities for self-regulation and motivation. You may need to prepare yourself physically by accumulating the tools and information you'll need; you may need to prepare yourself emotionally by building in support systems; and you may need to prepare yourself financially by obtaining funding or fellowships for the dissertation writing year.

41

Rather than being frustrated at all of the tasks that might seem to be taking away from your true work-that of writing the dissertation-consider, instead, that all the preparation might be a way to smooth the process. Certainly, if you expect to spend a few nights in the library over the next few weeks, getting all your laundry done early or your refrigerator stocked with food (or even cooking some meals ahead of time) are valid techniques for supporting your dissertation process.

Too often, graduate students feel guilty and uncomfortable about time spent away from the dissertation. That's why I recommend taking some time at the beginning of the process to prepare your life to let in the dissertation. Stock up on food, clean your living space, spend a little extra time with your partner or significant other; in other words, deposit some "extras" into the bank of your life and relationships so you have a bit extra to withdraw as needed.

Another step in preparing yourself to work on the dissertation is to take a realistic look at your schedule and to start to block out days/time for maintaining a balanced life. Rather than thinking about scheduling large blocks of time (six to eight hours, for example), start by scheduling one to two hours of work at a time. Give your body and mind a chance to adjust to working on the dissertation. Then, after a week or so, gradually shift this one- or two-hour block into something a bit longer, maybe three hours. Gradually increase your dissertation working time, but never allot more than five hours at a time. The literature on adult learning suggests that adults work best within time frames of forty-five to ninety minutes, and then require a break to retain productivity. You will benefit from shorter working periods that are more focused and productive. There is no value in sitting in front of the computer for five hours just because you think you should, when, in reality, you stopped working productively more than two hours ago. You will find the dissertation process much easier and more satisfying if you aim to get in, work hard, and then get out.

At the end of your working time, shift your focus and your attention. Get some lunch, pet your cat, go for a walk, visit your neighbors, anything that will help you shift away from the dissertation and immerse yourself in something else. To start, I recommend working on the dissertation no more than once per day for no more than three hours at a time. If you find it difficult to carve out this kind of time in one block, consider working on the dissertation two times a day for about an hour. You will be surprised at how much progress can be made in a tightly focused efficient hour.

Finally, as you keep moving through the process, take regular time outs to refresh and recharge. Use these breaks to catch up with your family and friends, maybe get ahead on some household chores, and, of course, to relax. It's almost like you will jump into the pool of the dissertation, swim around for a while, and then get out and dry off before diving back in again. Get comfortable with the idea of preparing yourself to dive back in, and you'll feel more secure in your mastery of this process.

Finding your optimum working style

Finding your optimum working style refers to finding a pattern of behaviors that consistently supports you in reaching your desired goals. Dissertation success is closely tied to consistency, so the more you can create workable routines, the better.

One way to create workable routines is to find a time each day that you commit to working on your dissertation. For those working full time, this might involve rising early a couple days a week so that you have a quiet hour to work before everyone else gets up. For those who are full-time mothers, you might find quiet time in the early morning or perhaps during your child's nap time or after s/he has gone to bed. The key is to find a time each day that is designated for your dissertation-and to make sure you work on the dissertation in that time. It's also important that you schedule in periodic rest breaks in the day. Avoid binge writing and binge relaxing. It's much better to work for a solid hour or two and then take a complete break than it is to work four so-so hours punctuated by procrastination and loss of focus.

It is best to start working in small increments and then gradually increase them. Too often, ABDs jump into the dissertation process by logging eight-hour or longer days of working on the paper. The problem with this approach is that you usually can't sustain this level of intensity for too long. It is better, much better, to work in shorter blocks consistently than it is to jump right into full days. The dissertation needs to be chipped away at, bit by bit. You want to consider it like a part-time job. You do your work, give it your all-and then you go on to something else.

Once you have begun to work on the dissertation frequently in small blocks of time, you will want to start adding in some structure/framework related to your methods for getting into and out of the work. When you are starting out, it can be relatively easy to slip into the work; most students can accommodate short working bursts of about fifteen to twenty minutes. However, as time goes on, your dissertation may require somewhat longer time frames (thirty to forty minutes, for example), and you may need to create some clear cues to settle into writing and then to leave it when the other demands of your life require your attention. It is difficult to make this shift too frequently, so you need structures to assist you.

One good technique during the writing phase is to leave your final sentence unfinished to be completed the next day. This makes it easier to pick up where you left off, which will smooth the transition into writing. I tend to recommend that ABDs not spend a lot of time reading what they wrote the day before. This can become a lengthy process and often results in rewriting what you already wrote rather than aiming to get a full draft written. Always aim to write new material before extensive rewriting of your work.

If you are in the organization or research phase, a good technique to help you get to work each day is to keep a running to-do list and mark what you will begin with on your next day of work. Make notes about where you will pick up on the next day. It's also helpful to list three to five tasks you will accomplish each day. Set goals for each day, and you find accomplishment is much easier.

When you are ready to leave your work for the day, I also suggest that you take a few minutes to straighten up your work area and to leave the space in good order so that you can get back to work the next day with a minimum of hassle and fuss. It also can be helpful to take a ten-minute transition between writing and getting back to your life. Use this time to jot down any ideas floating in your head, to take some notes for use later, or to just sit quietly until you need to rejoin the rest of the world. This type of transition can assist you in moving back smoothly into your life and other roles.

It also can be very motivating to use kind of visual aid to track your dissertation progress. My clients have used world maps and tracked their progress across the map with the aid of straight pins. Some have used jars filled with cookies (small ones); for every hour of dissertation work completed, they got to eat a cookie. This allowed them a taste of something sweet after finishing the work (which was reinforcing in itself)-and they were able to see the jar getting emptier and emptier for each hour spent on the dissertation. Other clients who didn't have a sweet tooth used marbles to track progress; for each hour spent on the dissertation, one marble was placed in the jar. Still another client decided to make a Hawaii jar (which was to be her reward to herself after defense), adding one glass bead each time she worked on the dissertation. You get the idea-some kind of visual tracking system (with or without cookies) can be helpful.

One other concept relevant to finding your optimum working style is the idea of honoring your natural rhythms. What this means is that you, within reason, try to work on the dissertation when you feel like working on it and then give yourself the space to choose not to work on it occasionally. It means that you find a time to work that feels good for you-early in the morning if you are up early, later at night if you stay up late. It also means that you still take care of your needs for food, sleep, and relaxation.

Conceptualizing the dissertation is not a linear process. Yes, sometimes, you need to force yourself to sit down and work through an idea. But sometimes, you might find the solution you seek in another, easier way. I have heard numerous stories from ABDs who left the computer and went to plant flowers and then had a breakthrough for the dissertation while they were digging in the dirt. I believe strongly in the inherent internal wisdom that we each possess, which some would call intuition or "inner knowing." I suggest that at those times where your heart, mind, and soul are calling out for something different from sitting at the computer, you should give into this desire for about thirty minutes. See what a difference this can make in your working style and how you feel about the dissertation.

By finding your optimum working style and honoring your rhythms, you will also decrease dramatically the feelings and behaviors that lead to procrastination and avoidance within the dissertation process. So, in all likelihood, you'll actually end up achieving more.

What are the some of the procrastination and avoidance behaviors you need to watch out for?

•Can't settle down to write. In this behavior, you feel like there are hundreds of other items that need to be dealt with before you can sit down to write. Or, you actually do sit down to write, but then spring up out of your chair because you need to do laundry or pick some flowers. A method for easing into the writing was discussed in the previous chapter. Another way to ease into writing is to, ahead of time, create a very detailed outline (some of my clients term it "excruciatingly detailed") and use this as a lever to move you into writing. At first, you might start by writing to the outline. Then, after a time, you will find your thinking/writing begin to open up and become richer. So, having an outline can be helpful if you believe you can't just sit down and write.

• Fear. Many ABDs worry about the end point before they've even begun. They worry about whether what they have written is correct and they often try to get to the end without going through the process. Writing is messy. Creation is messy. Creating new knowledge in the dissertation is messy. The sooner you accept this and understand that it's a necessary part of the process, the more quickly you will let go of the fear of failing at it. As much as possible, stay focused on today, not where you will be a week or a month from now. Don't worry about how you will defend your argument during your defense; get the argument written first, and remember that it will go through a few revisions before making it into the final product. Try to remember that this is a learning process for you, not one in which you are expected to know it all.

• Strong dislike for working. Some of my clients have described the dissertation process as very painful. And no wonder. They sit in tiny rooms on hard, uncomfortable chairs. They are cut off from life (and other people) and are left to battle their internal critics all on their own. For clients who are dreading the dissertation, I suggest that they find other places such as a nearby coffee shop to work or I encourage them to make an agreement with another dissertator to meet up and sit together as they each work on their own writing. I encourage my clients to read articles sitting outside in the sun or by the pool, and I encourage them to brighten their working spaces with live plants, fresh flowers, wind chimes, or whatever else makes the space feel alive. It's much more difficult to dread the work when you're doing it in pleasant surroundings.

• Doubts about your ability. This is a tough one, and you may want to reread the chapter on negative self talk. If you find yourself caught in a cycle of perpetual doubts and a resulting inability to produce, you may want to look at the number and kind of social supports you have. My guess would be you don't have enough. You may want to find more people who can support you, whether they are professionals (therapist, coach) or peers (writing group, e-mail lists), or mentors/advisers (at your school or others). Chronic self-doubt can be debilitating. If you have occasional self-doubt, remind yourself that you wouldn't have gotten this far if you didn't have what it takes to finish the degree.

•Impatience. This behavior is closely tied to fear of failure and perfectionism. Feeling impatient with the process means that your expectations are unrealistic for the current situation. And if they remain so, it also means that this whole process is going to be much more painful than it must be. If you feel extremely impatient with the process, you might need to find other ways to burn off some of this excess energy. Consider going for a run or engaging in a tough workout. Such options will help release stress and impatience as well as endorphins, the body's feel-good chemicals that can take the edge off. If you are more internally impatient, you can try shifting to another part of the work that might be easier to accomplish. Some days, though, you will not be able to push through to the next level. If you've tried to do so and it's just not working, it can be better to do some other kind of work such as editing or revising for a while to see if that helps. Impatience can also mean that you are feeling driven by some external forces or developments that you might need to examine in more detail so you can work through them and let them go.

•Anger, annoyance, resentment. These feelings tend to crop up in one of two situations. They can occur because you've forgotten that the dissertation is a choice. Rather than remembering why you are doing this (remember chapter 1), you've gotten stuck in believing that you have no choice about whether or how to do this. If this describes you, it would be a good idea to go back to the start of the book and think about why you're doing this project. You might find that your reasons and motivation have changed, and that's okay. Recommit to the process and get moving again-or decide that you don't want the degree and move on. I don't mean to sound like it's an easy decision-it's not-but really, those ultimately are your only two choices. Either you're going to finish it or not, and it will be now or not. That's it.

A second reason for anger, annoyance, or resentment comes when you have recently received evaluation or feedback on your work product. Your adviser might have told you to write something and then asked you to take out what you just spent hours writing. You might feel upset over how much you're sacrificing for the project or you might feel resentful at how slow the process can be some-times. Whatever the reason, you need to find a way to get these feelings dealt with and out of your way. If you don't, they will slowly leach away your motivation and energy to do this project. And, again, once that happens, you need to decide to finish, or decide not to. I have worked with sev-eral people who were in ABD limbo for more than ten years. Please don't do that to yourself. It's not worth it. If you find that your negative feelings are overwhelming you, look to increase the number of social supports in your life through connecting with a therapist, coach, peers, and mentors/advisers. Remember, there are no extra points for suffering.

Patience is a virtue

Many important achievements in life take time to complete. Babies take nine months to be born. Relationships take months or years to develop. Getting into a Ph.D. program in the first place took twenty years of schooling.

The dissertation process, like these other processes, takes time. The more comfortable you can be with the time required to finish it and the more you can manage your frustrations and urgency in an appropriate manner, the easier you will find it to finish.

As I've already mentioned, working steadily on the dissertation will allow you to make significant progress. While not nearly as dramatic and emotional as binge writing and binge avoidance, in the dissertation, as in the fable of the tortoise and the hare, slow and steady wins the race. If you can relax into the process and move ahead in a consistent-though perhaps not always exciting-way, you will be much better off than those students who work in cycles and burn themselves out too early.

The dissertation process is a test of fortitude and patience. If you've ever taken part in building a house, you know that the process at first doesn't look like much. A group of surveyors come and plot out the foundation, and then the foundation is dug. After this, the walls are staked out and concrete is mixed and poured. At this point, the workers have little idea what the finished product will look like, but they show up to work every day, taking small steps toward the finished product. While houses are built from a master plan (and the dissertation process should have some broad brushstroke type of plan as well), in houses as in dissertations, you have to show up every day to meet the goal—even when it isn't exactly clear when you'll reach it. House builders generally give estimates of time to completion, allowing time for unexpected events, and they keep working (hopefully) until the work is done. The same kind of process needs to be structured into your life for your dissertation. You need to show up for work every day, even when the end point doesn't seem that clear or certain.

It is always better to do even mediocre work consistently than it is to do brilliant work inconsistently. Graduate students who wait for the Muse to visit before working on the project tend to be ABD for much longer than those who find a way to work on it in a consistent fashion. Inspiration and deep excitement and passion are not always necessary components to dissertation progress.

When scheduling in your dissertation work, it is most effective to set aside at least a bit of time to work each day. Many of my clients find it's most effective to work at the same time each day. This might be more feasible for students who are working on the dissertation full time (or close to it) or for those students who are able to schedule themselves with a great deal of certainty each day. For those who might be working full time at an outside job or who might have significant other responsibilities, it is optimal to set aside the same time each week to work on the project. For instance, you might set aside time every Tuesday and Thursday morning. If you are planning to finish your dissertation in twelve to eighteen months, you will need to produce about five pages of writing each week (or about one page per weekday) to meet this goal. This assumes chapters of twenty-five to thirty pages and that you are steadily producing output. What you may notice from this example is that five pages a week may feel doable. By thinking of the writing in five-page increments, you can see that the dissertation need not be a mysterious and looming project without structure or focus.

One of my clients, Megan*, really hooked on to this idea of five pages per week. Megan was aiming to work on the dissertation for about two to four hours each day. She was comfortably able to produce a page of writing on most days. She used a jar of marbles to track her progress, awarding herself one marble for each page written. At the end of two weeks, if she had at least eight marbles in the jar, she gave herself a reward. Not surprisingly, Megan finished ahead of schedule. She made good use of the strategies we've discussed so far, having a clear goal, using visual means to track her progress, and giving herself rewards along the way. The other interesting benefit was that Megan was able to work on the dissertation for the first part of the day, and spent the rest of the day going to the gym, seeing her friends and boyfriend, cooking, and relaxing. She had a clear goal and felt positive about her progress towards that goal and she, perhaps more than any other graduate student I've ever coached, was able to compartmentalize the dissertation as one task in her life, not her whole life. As a result, she was fairly balanced and happy throughout the entire process, and demonstrated patience with herself, the process, and the inevitable adjustments and revisions that were needed to finalize the project.

If you have not made significant progress on your dissertation lately, you might want to start small. You probably have heard something about the process of writing for fifteen minutes per day, as identified by Dr. Joan Bolker in her book *Write Your Dissertation in Fifteen Minutes a Day*. I agree with this approach, but sometimes recommend starting even smaller. If you are feeling stalled out, impatient, or stuck, it's best to start with the smallest possible increment that you can easily do. For some clients, this is just five minutes, or perhaps even one. If you consider that the dissertation is moved ahead by every minute you spend working on it, you will begin to appreciate the value of

Name has been changed.

even working one minute or five minutes. Again, it's not as sexy, dramatic, or exciting as the "write feverishly all night" approach, but the one- or five- or fifteen-minute chunk can still get the work done.

If you find yourself feeling distracted and unable to write, it might be because you are trying to write before the ideas are fully formed in your mind or because you're finding it difficult to express what you want to say. It can be difficult to remain patient with the idea incubation process. There are some techniques you can try to move the thinking process along a bit faster:

•Try speaking out loud about your thoughts and taping them into a tape recorder. When you listen back to the tape, you might be able to hear connections (or gaps) and have a better idea of how to address them. If you are a fast and accurate typist, you might even want to consider transcribing your spoken thoughts onto paper. This can help you overcome the starkness of a plain white sheet of paper that seems to be waiting-not always patiently-for your thoughts.

•Try writing down your topic areas in the form of questions. Instead of "Talk about so-and-so's contribution to XYZ," write, "What was so-and-so's contribution to the XYZ?" This technique comes from a process developed by Steve Manning, who has worked with many writers. Manning has found that it is much easier for a writer to begin writing on the answer to a question. This process may help you as well.

•Try talking about your ideas aloud to a peer, spouse, or partner. Sometimes, sharing our ideas with others can help us clarify our arguments. If your listener is willing, have him/her repeat back what was said and allow questions. This can demonstrate where the logic of your argument may be faltering or breaking down.

•Consider easing into the writing by starting with a section that you know you can easily handle, perhaps one in which you are merely reporting information rather than interpreting it.

•Finally, if you have tried some of the above but are still stuck, you might consider spending your working time in another form of necessary activity such as organization, additional research, revision, or editing. Sometimes, you just can't produce new writing on command.

If you are by nature an impatient, angry, or fast-paced person, you might find elements of the dissertation process worse than fingernails on a chalkboard. You may want to consider hiring help with your research, analysis, editing, or formatting, which can get the process moving more quickly. If this is not in your budget or doesn't appeal to you, you might try cultivating a more patient attitude by means of yoga, meditation, or similar practices. The concept of being patient in the dissertation means, ultimately, that you are fully present to what is happening right now. You are not spending the majority of your time moving back to the past (such as in writing and rewriting the same five pages or ruminating about your last meeting with your adviser), or moving into the future (worrying about where you will apply for jobs more than eighteen months from now or wondering what you'll wear your defense). The more patience you can cultivate in other parts of your life, the more this patience will spill over into the dissertation process, and this will assist you in maintaining the internal sense of balance and equilibrium necessary for this project.

Organizing your materials

One of the questions I'm most frequently asked is, "How should I organize my materials?" While no one process works for every person, let's discuss some that have been of value to ABD's I've coached.

•Think of it in sections. When you are researching your material, you want to have some sense, even if it's vague, about where the material will be best placed in your dissertation. At the start, you should have folders labeled with each section, topic, or theme you will be exploring. At first, obtain all the information needed for a particular topic or theme. Then, after reading and taking notes on the article, might move it to another folder labeled by chapter. It's wise to have a folder marked Supplemental Reading; in this folder will be articles that you might read if you have time or need further support for your point. These might also be termed "tertiary sources" or "not as relevant secondary sources," anything that keeps these less-needed articles out of the main piles. Eventually, you want to have all the research material separated out by relevant section so that you can be certain you have all you need when you turn to working on that section. Ideally, you will have a distinct research process and a well-developed plan by the time you get to the writing phase. It is very difficult to research and write at the same time, partly because it is difficult to productively shift mental gears in that fashion. So, as much as possible, aim to separate your material into relevant sections during the organization phase.

One type of organization you might try involves three-ring binders, dividers, and plastic sheet protectors. Let's say one binder is labeled as chapter 1. Gather the articles for that chapter and place them in appropriate sections. You might have scribbled notes on slips of paper; these will be placed into the plastic sheet protectors, and, if possible, assigned to a particular section of the chapter.

If I were working on a dissertation about automobiles, my chapter 1 binder might look like this:

Cover: Chapter I: Considerations for Automobile Design
   Section I: History of the automobile:
          Articles: who designed first automobile, what was the public reaction, what were the pre-automobile transportation options, how was the first design conceived, who did it, etc.

   Section II: What were early considerations for exterior design?
          Articles: who were the main designers of auto bodies? What were the materials used? Was this limited by materials available? Did early designs mimic any other form of transportation?

   Section III: What were early considerations for interior design?
          Articles: who designed early interiors? Were there choices? If so, what were they? What were the available materials? What was important to the consumers?

   Section IV: What were the factors influencing design?
          Articles: How did the economic climate influence design? Were designs borrowed from other countries? How did the designs change for the U.S. market?

Now, you're not always going to get very neat divisions for

this information, but do the best you can. If an article can be used in more than one place, put it in the earliest section first. You can always move it to a later one if needed. Also, note in this example that I used many questions to determine the content of each section.

You can do the same thing for your own sections. For each chapter, write out the questions you might answer in it so you know best how to divide up the articles. You can do this by brainstorming a list of twenty to twenty-five questions about who, what, why, where, when, and how. This can give you a starting point for developing the chapter sections.

Another question I'm asked very often is how many articles should be obtained for each major point. In my estimation, three to five sources are a good starting number. If you have three to five sources for every major point, you should in most cases have all that you need to write a solid dissertation. When you go to the library or request materials be sent to you, have some general idea about what section these materials might go into. Some students request numerous articles focused on a single aspect, which creates an unnecessary amount of paper that must be waded through and organized. By staying focused on where you believe the article will fit, you will find it easier to define the end point of the research process.

When organizing your materials, create a filing process that diminishes the number of times you must handle an article before using it. It is better to set up an overly detailed organization process than one that does not provide the full range of information needed. With my clients, I recommend another step to the three-ring binder organization process, one that involves using colored pens or markers.

If you have set up your articles in a three-ring binder and divided them up by sections, you can now move onto the next step, color coding each section (such as section I in red) and putting a mark of that color at the top right corner of all articles belonging to this section of the dissertation. You might want to mark it with a 1, to signify chapter 1 as well. If an article will cover multiple sections, mark it in two colors so you know where else it might be needed. Color coding in this way helps you identify on sight where each article should go, and it will helps you later to construct a bibliography and clean up your citations if needed.

As we are currently focusing on article organization, another way to organize your materials is to consider investing in bibliographic software. Consider the program Endnote at http://www.endnote.com. I don't get any benefit from recommending this program, but my clients have found it useful and it doesn't seem that all graduate students know about it. In any case, bibliographic software, obtained early on, can simplify the research and organization process and keep you from ordering the same article multiple times, because you can scan the list of articles in your database and avoid obtaining duplicates.

Some clients have complained about the time that organizing materials can take. I agree; it can take a long time, though it has been my experience that the time is well spent. When you don't have to worry about maintaining your articles in a particular order as you read them (because the color coding will help you know where they should be refiled), you free yourself up to the creative process of writing.

As you reach the end of a particular section or chapter, it's valuable to take a few minutes to scan the contents of your catchall file. It's common to find useful information that can be added with a minimum of fuss. This file can also be a place to restimulate your thinking about this section or the next one. So, it's helpful periodically to scan the contents of this collection and use, refile, or throw away the items as appropriate.

Once you have completed a section or chapter, it's good to take a few minutes to refile and clean out any information you won't need again in the immediate future. Cull through the binder to find any information that should be moved or filed into another binder. Put the binder away on a shelf or bookcase. This can create a sense of completion and division as you move through the parts of the dissertation. Take the time to prune down your articles on a regular basis, filing away those that you won't need or that turned out to be tangential or irrelevant. This focus on consistently cleaning out your space can keep you from becoming overwhelmed by paper and feeling uncertain or confused about whether you covered everything you had planned to discuss.

Creating a
work space that works

As you set up or rearrange your existing work space to accommodate your dissertation, there are several factors that you will want to address to create favorable working conditions. These factors include ergonomic considerations, location/placement considerations, flexibility in your working style, and creation of an environment that supports your particular way of working. We'll discuss each of these in more detail.

From an ergonomic perspective, you will want to make sure that your desk or table is at the appropriate height for you to work comfortably. According to the Environmental Health and Public Safety Center (EHPSC) at North Carolina State University (http://www.ncsu.edu/ehs/www99/right/handsMan/office/ergonomic.html), your desk should be at such a height that you can keep a 90- to 100-degree elbow angle and straight wrists when you type. It's recommended that your work space be at least thirty by sixty inches, large enough to accommodate all of your computer equipment as well as other working materials. If you have an existing work space that does not conform to these requirements, you can manage the height issue by creative use of a chair and footrest. If your desk surface is less than the recommended size, consider creating a larger work space by adding a table or additional desk in an L-shaped configuration or create a desktop configuration that allows you to move the computer out of the way during the times where you need more flat working space for outlining articles or reading a book).

The EHPSC further recommends that the seat of your chair be placed sixteen to twenty-five inches off the floor so that your feet are flat on the floor, thighs parallel to the floor, and your arms at a 90-degree angle for typing.

A chair with rounded front edges and support, particularly in the lower back region, is recommended. Above all, the chair should allow easy access into and out of the working space and should not impair the user's ability to sit comfortably at the desk. Consider obtaining a chair with castors (rollers) so you can move easily about the space if needed. A plastic chair mat can both protect the floor and keep you from straining your legs as you move the chair about the office.

Lighting is another important consideration. If possible, you will want to have several lighting options. Natural light and a window can be useful if you like sunlight, and they certainly can make the dissertation process feel less sterile. A desk lamp is useful as well. It's also important to make sure that there is enough ambient light coming into the work space; your eyes can feel more strained more quickly if the computer monitor is the only source of light in the room.

As you arrange your work space, you want to have room to keep your reference materials nearby, perhaps in a bookshelf or on a table. The more efficient your work space and the more motion you can conserve, the easier it will be for you. If you have a printer with a paper tray at the bottom, get a printer/fax table or some item that will allow you to easily open and replace the paper tray. You likely will be printing many items, so you want to set up the printer in such a way so that it remains easy to use and highly functional over the long term.

When you are arranging your work space, it's also important to consider your natural style of working. Are you a person who does everything sitting at your desk? Or do you read articles curled up in a chair and then use your desk only for computer work? Whatever your style is, it's important to set up your office in a way that works for you. During my dissertation process, I found that I liked to read articles while sitting on the couch, so I moved a two-drawer rolling file cabinet there to keep articles handy. Whenever I had a few minutes, I could easily pull out an article and do some work in a way that was most comfortable for me. Since I was also working as a full-time clinical intern when completing my paper, it was important to me that I spend the least amount of time sitting at a desk as I possibly could, since I did that for most of my workday. If you like to read in bed, keep a small file box or drawer next to your bed. While this might not be in keeping with the recommendations for good sleep hygiene, if you are going to read in bed anyway, you might as well make it easy and effortless to do so.

Remember, not all work has to happen at your computer. Some of my clients have enjoyed reading articles at the park or at a coffeehouse. They've enjoyed writing the dissertation on a laptop by the water. They've met at each other's houses to work alone, but together. If you find yourself dreading some aspect of the dissertation, try changing your working place for that activity. In fact, the more you dread a particular dissertation activity, the more enjoyable I want your environment to be. If you hate that feeling of being cooped up writing while the world is passing you by, then take your work outside and sit on the patio or deck so you can be surrounded by fresh air and birds. There is nothing that says your dissertation will be that much better because you suffered inside on a nice day. Again, there are no extra bonuses for suffering in this process.

As you define and create a supportive work environment, make keeping it clutter-free one of your highest priorities.

Many people find it difficult to write when surrounded by too much visual clutter. In the book *Writing in Flow*, author Susan Perry interviewed hundreds of writers who all said essentially the same thing: a plain, almost drab, visual environment is the most useful for finding flow in the writing process. Many of the writers were quoted as saying they had boring views and plain walls in their writing nooks, almost as if to make the environment so plain that they had no choice but to write. I advocate a layout that falls somewhere between the two, one that is plain enough that you aren't distracted away from writing but that also is appealing enough that you enjoy being there. The balance is up to you to create, based on your own personal preferences and circumstances. No matter what you do, remember that creating a work space that works can mean the difference between working on the dissertation and avoiding it completely.

If you for whatever reason don't have the luxury of a separate work space, then consider creating a portable/rolling office using some of these ideas:

• Find (or obtain) a large table surface for your work. A kitchen or formal dining room table can work well.

• Obtain a filing cabinet that can be stored in your garage or attic or in the corner of the room. This will be the primary storehouse for the dissertation material you're not actively using.

• Get two two-drawer rolling carts-one with file drawers and the other with regular drawers. Use the cart with filing drawers to store the articles and materials you're actively using or to hold the binder you made of articles. Use the other cart to store reference materials, office supplies, and so forth. If you are using a laptop, you can also store it on top of one of these carts when it's not in use.

When it is time to work on your dissertation, you can roll

the carts into the space, set up the laptop, and get to work. When it's time to stop for the day, you can easily and quickly pack up all your materials and roll them out of the way until they are next needed. With all of the storage and organizational options available today, you can easily create a working space that fits your space and budget constraints. Again, setting up an efficient work space can take time, but the satisfaction you will gain from a well-run office will more than make up for it over the course of the dissertation process.

Ideas for controlling clutter

During the dissertation process, it's inevitable that some amount of clutter will accumulate in your work space. Sometimes, this clutter will be clips of articles, scribbled ideas, or just information that you think it would be good to save but don't yet know exactly why.

It's a good idea to sort and re-sort your existing piles periodically to make sure you are including all relevant information for a particular chapter. As you finish a writing milestone (such as the end of a chapter), it's a good idea to take a bit of time and clean out papers and information for which you won't have immediate use.

When you decide to de-clutter, you will want to think about clutter from several perspectives. First, you will want to think about where to focus your efforts. Where can you de-clutter that will make the most significant positive impact on your dissertation process? Do you have a pile of papers blocking the door that annoys you every time you enter or leave the room? If so, you might start there. Begin with piles or areas that are particularly troublesome.

Next, you might sift all your papers and articles into appropriate piles, by chapter as I recommend or by theme, which can be a bit unwieldy. If you don't know where an article or paper should go, put it in a clear plastic folder or sleeve. You'll sort through this periodically and clean it out, too.

Take small steps. Focus on cleaning up one area at a time and take care that perfectionism and procrastination don't show up disguised as a cleaning frenzy. Give yourself a time limit in which to complete the tasks.

Resist the temptation to read everything as you put it away. The only articles you should read or even skim right now are the ones that are most immediately relevant. If you are not sure, put the article aside in a separate pile to refer to later. This process should result in a pile of articles and material for each chapter as well as a pile to skim later. If you resist the temptation to read as you go, de-cluttering will happen more quickly and with less anxiety.

Finally, another way to control clutter is to make sure you only get enough information-not too much. If you have about three to five sources for each major point, this is usually enough. Take the best sources and leave the rest. You don't need fifteen citations to make your point.

Creating
good work habits

As I've discussed, having good work habits will significantly increase your rate of progress on the dissertation. Based
on my experience, there are several work habits that can
assist you in reaching your goals.

•Work every day. This may not be possible for everyone.
But the fastest way to finish is to work on the dissertation
at least fifteen to twenty minutes per day. This will not
always involve writing or editing, but also can involve tasks
such as returning phone calls, entering data, obtaining a
few articles, taking notes, thinking about an idea, outlining
your next steps, and adding to your to-do list. You could
even count the few minutes you spend reading this book.
I encourage all of my clients to consider all the dissertation-
related actions they take as part of the total time worked.
There appears to be some fallacy that all the preparation
work doesn't matter, that only writing really counts. I dis-
agree; the writing couldn't happen if the preparation work
hadn't been done in the first place. So, whatever time you
spend in activities directly related to the dissertation, consider that time spent working on the process. This can help
you overcome the feeling that you need large, uninterrupted blocks of time to accomplish anything meaningful.
Sometimes, the more large blocks of time you have, the
less productive you really are. We all work most optimally
when we have forty five to fifty minute blocks of work fol-
lowed by about ten to fifteen minutes of rest. The more you

can make progress in small, "found" blocks of time, the better. Open your mind to this possibility and get creative.

One client, Jeremy*, took this idea and ran with it. He created a running list of actions that he could accomplish in five minutes or less. As you might imagine, his list was sometimes very detailed. He was balancing the dissertation with a family and a full-time job, so the five-minute blocks worked really well for him. He was able to find a couple of five-minute chunks before lunchtime, using the time to order articles, return calls, or look up a reference or citation. These small bits of progress fueled his motivation and momentum. He began to make a game of seeing how many five-minute items he could cross off each week. An additional benefit of this approach was that he used his time very wisely during the week so, when the weekend came, he was able to sit and write for a few hours on Saturday morning because he had already read, organized, and thought through what he wanted to say during the week. He completed his paper in just about eleven months. Staying in focused, directed motion, even for five minutes at a time, quickly adds up.

Another aspect of creating good work habits is the capacity to compartmentalize your dissertation from other parts of your life. When you are working on the project, work on it. When you're not, go out and do other things. Take advantage of your best writing times as often as possible, and then go and live your life. Treat the dissertation as a part-time job: you work on it sometimes, and then you leave it when you go on to other activities or tasks. Again, more hours of time do not always equate to higher output or quality. I'd rather you make two or three hours of solid progress than six to eight hours of so-so or no progress. You don't need to give up your life to do the dissertation. You do need to find a way to bring it into your life and create a dynamic balance between it and your other areas of focus and responsibility.

*Name has been changed.

69

As you've probably already noticed, more hours of work don't necessary mean greater output and higher quality. Most people find that they make more progress, more easily when they are juggling a reasonable number of commitments at once. This might seem counterintuitive. Shouldn't you be able to complete the greatest amount of dissertation work when you have nothing to do except the dissertation? This seems like it would make sense, but the truth is that it rarely seems to work out that way. Why is this? I think it relates to the fact that it is difficult to remain focused exclusively on one task for this length of time. You have too much time to think, rethink, and go back over ground you've already covered. When your dissertation is the only item looming in your calendar, it is difficult to feel motivated. Most people find that they make more progress on their dissertations when their working time is limited by other commitments or responsibilities, especially when these other focuses-such as part-time jobs and planned time with friends-can be anticipated and completed on schedule. It is more difficult, though not impossible, to juggle less "plannable" type of responsibilities such as children and unexpected family events. By having other areas of life to focus on, you will be more likely to make good use of the dissertation time you do have. Remember the saying, "Work expands to fill the time allotted to it." Within reason, the less time you allot, the more efficiently you are likely to complete your work in the time allotted.

Another aspect of creating good work habits is that you are able to focus on keeping your scheduled work time as productive as possible. This means that all your preparation work (sharpening pencils, skimming articles, making notes, color coding your socks) needs to happen before you sit down to write. It is best to work in forty-five- to fifty-minute blocks of time and then follow each block with a ten- to fifteen-minute rest break. If you can get yourself into the rhythm of working forty-five to fifty minutes at a time, and then taking ten to fifteen minutes to wander outside, pet the dog or cat, get a drink of water, or fix yourself something to eat, then you will be able to see progress very quickly. When you refuse to allow yourself to sink into the flow of your work due to outside distractions and mini-breaks, you drag the working time out and begin to procrastinate and avoid getting into the work later on because you feel that you're running out of time to create anything meaningful. Instead, get everything you need to work productively for a forty-five-minute stretch. Consider setting a timer if needed. If forty-five minutes is too much to start with, set smaller goals, such as a fifteen- or twenty-minute block. The most important aspect is to work efficiently when you're working and to try to accomplish as much as you can in each sitting. For example, in writing this book, I planned where I wanted to be by the end of each segment. By setting mini-goals along the way and writing this book at the rate of five pages per day, I was able to maintain a steady working pace and to meet my goal of completing this volume in just one month of daily writing. Writing in five-page page bursts also felt extremely doable to me, and it was gratifying to see that I had about thirty-five to thirty-seven pages written at the end of the first week, and that the manuscript grew longer and longer each week.

It's important to add new habits slowly. If you have not worked on your dissertation regularly, it's unrealistic to think you're going to move directly from zero hours of work per day to eight uninterrupted hours of work. Planning your work in this way sets you up for binge writing (or binge avoidance), and then feelings of anger, guilt, worry, and strain as you fail to meet your goal. You then set an even larger goal the next time, and fail to meet it as well. You then start to look for an outside motivator, such as a meeting with your adviser. But since you haven't trained properly by using short, productive working segments, you aren't properly conditioned to take part in the longer writing bursts that will be necessary to meet your new, often unrealistic, deadline. Allow me to suggest again that, in this case, less is more. Again, it's better to work twenty minutes per day consistently than it is to work eight hours one day per month. If you can only work on the dissertation two times per week, build up slowly, and consider breaking your work up into several smaller chunks. Let's say that you work thirty minutes and then break for an hour and then work thirty more minutes or that you work thirty minutes in the morning and thirty minutes in the evening. The idea is to start with the smallest unit that is comfortably possible-the one where you say, "Oh, that's nothing!"-and to build up from there.

If you are doing a great deal of work on the computer, remember to make regular backups and copies of your work along the way. I didn't do this, and my computer died about a third of the way through my dissertation process. While I had copious notes and eventually (painfully) reconstructed everything, I could have saved myself a ton of grief if I'd just instituted a regular practice of backing my data up every week or every other week. This falls under the category of creating good work habits because you can never know when your computer might fail, and it's best to be prepared. Set your word processing program to "auto-save" every five to ten minutes. If your computer loses power suddenly, you will never have lost more than five to ten minutes of work. If you are using Microsoft Word, you can set this by going to Toolsà OptionsàSave-à AutoRecover info.

One last point about creating good work habits: don't worry so much about what other people do. Find what works best for you and stick with it. Everyone approaches this process differently; what works for one person may or may not work for another. With any of the information presented in this book or any information you read anywhere else, feel free to modify it to suit your own particular circumstance. Keep in mind the basic suggestions or points and then use the information to design the processes and systems that work best for you.

Maximizing your progress

Whether you're just getting started on the dissertation or have been working on it for a while, there will come a time that you will need to feel more motivated and/or like you're maximizing your progress. There are several means to do this: regular breaks, rewards, success journals, support systems, and interests outside the dissertation process.

Regular breaks in the dissertation progress are a useful strategy for maximizing progress. Again, this might sound counterintuitive, but let's use an analogy from weight lifting. When you regularly lift weights, and then take a break for a while, you very often come back stronger after the break. The break gives your body time to build up strength and create a reserve. A similar process can be thought to occur in the dissertation. When you have been working steadily and consistently and you plan regular breaks, you know that you have earned them. Very often, graduate students will say, "I'm afraid if I take a break that I'll never get back to work." If this is you, it may mean that you know you're not working as much as you could be. So, you need to work a bit more or ratchet down your goals. Or it may mean that you haven't really allowed yourself a break away from the dissertation in the first place. A regular break need not be overly complex or extremely involved. It may mean a half day off every week, or it may mean that you don't do dissertation work on Sundays. It may mean that you build in time to visit with your friends or to spend time with your spouse or significant other, any activity that feels like a break to you. It can be particularly refreshing to spend your break absorbed in a creative, right-brain kind of activity such as painting, drawing, working in clay, or even coloring. This gives your brain a chance to process more fully and to build up some reserve so you might come back to the dissertation process with fresh insights and new approaches.

Rewards are another means to maximize your dissertation progress. Strangely, most ABDs do not think well of rewards. In working with my coaching clients, we sometimes talk about the idea of rewards, as in rewarding yourself when you accomplish something. What's interesting is that while most people understand that rewards feel good, very few ABDs seem to take the time to reward themselves for their successes.

Most ABDs seem to feel they shouldn't need rewards, and so they allow all the small and-sometimes even the big-successes to go by unacknowledged and perhaps not fully appreciated. They seem to be always focused on the next big thing rather than celebrating and appreciating where they are and how far they've already come.

What comes to mind when you think about rewards? Do you think "maybe someday" or "I don't need them" or "maybe when my dissertation gets to X place"? I'd encourage you to review all of your goals for the next two months and to attach rewards to successful attainment or completion. For example, you might decide when you'll complete the next piece of the research or writing process and what reward you will take when you do so. It doesn't matter what the reward is, but it is important to actually link your achievements to your best rewards-and to actually give yourself the rewards you've promised.

Most people tend to walk around feeling underappreciated. This is in part because few of us take the time to appre-

ciate ourselves. We wait for external ac
and approval, but rarely take the time to 1
port ourselves. You will maximize your pro
clear goals with well-defined reward for
goals. Rewarding yourself along the way
dissertation process much sweeter-and who
fit from that?

Another tool for maximizing your success is that of keeping a success journal, a place where you track all the successes in your dissertation process and life.

I strongly recommend that all my clients keep a success
journal. As the name implies, a success journal is a place to
record all your wins and achievements, no matter how big
or small. In a process is lengthy as the dissertation, it's easy
to forget your wins and achievements along the way.

I recommend obtaining a notebook or other bound journal
so that you're able to keep all of your notes in the same
place. Each day, you'll jot down all the successes you had
in all areas of your life. On some days the list will be quite
simple, including items like: "I worked on my dissertation
for fifteen minutes." On other days, the list may be more in
depth or complex, including items like "I figured out the
central theme or main argument of this chapter" or "I successfully outlined the remaining points that are needed."

Of course, as I said the success journal can include items
from all areas of your life-in fact, the more areas you
include, the more successes you have. It's fun to review
your success journal and remind yourself of all your
achievements along the way. Spending a few minutes
looking back over your wins can serve as a mini-motiva-
tional boost to help you get over an obstacle or block.
Some days, your entry might read something like, "Worked
on the dissertation even though I hated it." This, too, might
be considered a success. It's important to keep track of all
that you do along the way so that you have a success jour-

to refer back to whenever you doubt that you're making progress. The success journal is a simple process that can lead to big gains in your own level of confidence and sense of capability.

If you don't yet have a success journal, I encourage you to start one today. I also encourage you to jot down all your successes, no matter how small or insignificant your critical mind judges them to be. I believe that you get what you focus on, so the more you focus on success, the more success you will get.

Another significant method for maximizing your dissertation progress is to create and maintain strong support systems. It is best, in my experience, to have both academic and personal support people in place. The academic support people might be your adviser, your mentor, your peers, a writing group, and colleagues who have recently completed their dissertations. What you are aiming for in creating an academic support system is to have a well-rounded team of people who have "been there, done that" regarding various aspects of the dissertation. It's best to recruit these team members early on, though it's also never too late to seek out more support. It's also wise to have a couple people on your team who are better at various dissertation tasks than you are-for example, someone who is really skilled with statistics, and someone who is really skilled with editing. These people can provide invaluable expertise and input on any challenges you might be experiencing. If you are lucky enough to have a close relationship with your adviser, s/he may be another source of support, helping you grow as an academician as you further develop as a scholar.

It is just as important to create a personal support system of people who support you and your happiness, whether or not they understand or support the dissertation process. Your personal support system may include your parents, siblings, other relatives, childhood friends, significant other, spouse-anyone who can provide love and under-standing without condition or reservation. The great thing about your personal support team is that they can help remind you of your abilities and capacities to complete this project, they can provide love and support when the going gets tough, and they can give you understanding and warmth and a venue to talk about something besides the dissertation.

It's important to create both an academic support team and a personal support team. Some overlap between the two is fine. Just make sure you have some people with whom you can talk about your personal feelings and some people with whom you can talk about dissertation challenges. It's best to not have these be all the same people all the time. You will experience your relationships as more meaningful and supportive if you don't overburden just one or two people with both your personal feelings and your disserta-tion challenges. This can be overwhelming for those not in the process, and can result in you not feeling as supported or heard as you might otherwise be.

If you don't have at least five support people in place-at least two academic and two personal, plus a significant other or family member-you will want to make that your first priority, as you will be able to maximize your disserta-tion progress when you have people supporting and assist-ing you along the way.

One other advantage of having a strong personal support system is that the more personal supports you have, the more likely you are to have a life outside of the dissertation process. It's quite common, especially early on, to feel con-sumed by the dissertation and the process can easily become the main focus of your life. Having friends and loved ones who are not in graduate school and who are not working on their dissertations naturally guarantees that you will have other areas to focus on aside from the dis-sertation. This is good. Again, as I've already mentioned, it works best for you to treat the dissertation like a part-time job. You work on it, make some progress, and then you go home and leave it until the next day. If you have a rich social life, you will find it much easier to keep the dissertation in perspective as one part of your life, not the whole thing.

As you move through the process, you are likely to experience occasional difficulties with time management and balancing your social life with your dissertation work. At times, you might be overwhelmed with a lot of social activity (like at the holidays or on days of religious observance) and times when you are overly focused on your dissertation. You want to try to reach an important dissertation milestone just before a planned social activity so that you can relax and enjoy yourself with a minimum of guilt. For times when you have spent a significant amount of time on the dissertation and feel like you want to spend time with your friends, consider taking one day off every few weeks. Plan these days into your calendar ahead of time, and when the day comes, go. Don't delay pleasure indefinitely; if you do, that will make the dissertation process pretty dreary and boring.

Goal setting/planning /time management

While we touched on the idea of time management as it relates to your social life, this chapter will focus on goal setting, planning, and time management as aids to completing the dissertation more quickly and easily.

First, set SMART goals. A SMART goal is one that is Specific, Measurable, Attainable, Realistic, and Timely. How do you know if your goals fit each of these criteria? Let's define each criterion a bit more fully.

Specific refers to how detailed the goal is. The more detailed and defined the goal is, the more likely it will meet this criterion. Let's take an example: "I will work on my dissertation tomorrow." Contrast that with: "I will work on section II of this chapter tomorrow for at least thirty minutes." Can you see how the second version is more specific?

Measurable refers to whether the outcome of the goal can be measured. Most graduate students think of goal measurement in quantities that are too large to promote successful goal attainment. Stated another way, the measurement bar is routinely set too high, which sets you up for failure. A measurement should always be of a quantity that you feel you can easily do. In fact, it's better to set a goal with a smaller measurement-five pages instead of ten, for example-because you can always surpass the goal if you like. An appropriately measured goal may be set in terms of time spent working or in terms of output (number of pages completed or number of notes taken or articles read).

Attainable refers to whether the goal is something you can achieve in the first place. This very often is based on an intuitive, or "felt" sense. If you set a goal that is too difficult, you will find that your motivation is likely to dip sharply. If it's too easy, you might find yourself procrastinating. Your task, as in the children's story about Goldilocks and the three bears, is to find a goal that is just right-not too difficult, not too easy.

Realistic refers to whether the goal can be completed in the time frame allotted or within the circumstances that currently exist. It is probably not realistic to think that you will complete the whole dissertation in a week. It is more realistic to think that you can complete the dissertation in a year or less. If you consistently feel some kind of pressure or discomfort about the goals you set, that might be a clue that your goals are not realistic for your current circumstances. Avoid setting unrealistic goals wherever you can; you'll be much happier and find that the process proceeds at a more even pace.

Timely refers to how significant the goal is at this time. Is it absolutely the most important aspect on which to focus now? Or is this a goal that can wait for a while? Sometimes, you might need to work on goals in certain order because later steps depend on earlier ones. Timeliness refers to ascertaining which goals are next to be met and which goals will give you the greatest return on your investment at this point in time. This is an effective concept to keep in mind when you find yourself being distracted and chasing down footnotes or other sources. Get in the habit early on of asking yourself, "Is this the most important thing I need to focus on?" If the answer is yes, get to it. If the answer is no, find out what is most important and get started on that.

If you continually focus on the next most important area to work on, you will find it much easier to keep yourself on task to the process. This gives your mind a place to focus and, in this focus, you will find that your dissertation progress is more direct and clearer, with fewer tangents, distractions, and feelings of wasted time.

Planning backward is an effective method for setting appropriate deadlines. When you plan backward, you are setting mini-goals for your progress in a day or week. Let's say that you have eight sections for chapter 1. If you want to finish this chapter in eight weeks, you have to write at the rate of one section per week. If you ever fall short of this number, you will need to pick up the pace to meet your deadline. If you are ever ahead of this goal, you can plan days off without sacrificing your dissertation progress. Most graduate students think of the dissertation as a "for-ward only" type of process, where they keep working forward and waiting for the magical moment when they are suddenly done. It can be frustrating and uncomfortable to keep working toward a goal that is not specific enough and is not timely. Instead, think about your dissertation in "chunks" or chapters and plan backward to reach your goals in a timely fashion.

You can also use this planning backward method when you are planning to complete your dissertation in time for a particular graduation day. You can see how to do that by working through the outline below. Remember to replace the dates given with those relevant for your school and your circumstances.

How to create a timeline to dissertation completion:

1) Start at the bottom #, listing when the dissertation is due in your department.
2) Work backward, using the time frames in the sample below, to create your target dates.
3) Once you have created your target dates,

work forward, by setting goals to span from the place where you are now to where you will be at your first target date.

Start proposal and Human Subjects Application
  (if Human Subjects applicable)
       (2 months)
	Aug 15

Send proposal to committee for review (1 month)	Oct 15

Send application for Human Subjects Review
       (if applicable)
       (after proposal accepted)
	Nov 15

Start collecting data or writing chapters (start here, allot 3 months)	Dec 15
Start data analysis, review of results (1 month)	Mar 15
Start writing discussion section, completed by (1 month)	Apr 15
Start writing conclusions and final Chapter (1 month)	May 15
Turn paper into committee for review (1 month)	Jun 15
Corrections and revisions based on feedback (2 weeks)	July 15
Prepare for defense (2 weeks)	Aug 1
Defense	Aug 15*

This is intended as a sample only; actual dates and dead-lines will vary based on your department.

It can be highly effective to plan backward for each chapter and to set weekly and daily goals for your dissertation work. If you choose to try this approach, you'll need to have certain pieces of information already in place.

Let's say that you want to plan backward to complete chapter 3 by June 15. In the model above, we are allotting about six weeks per chapter, but we haven't planned what you will do in that six-week time frame. For simplicity's sake, let's say that you have six sections to write for this chapter. You will need to finish about one section per week to make your deadline. If you wanted to break it down further, you could determine how much you'd need to accomplish each day to reach your goal. Let's say that you worked on the first third of the section on days one and two, and then the next third on days three and four, and the final third on days five and six. Can you see how, in this method, each of your days would be planned in complete alignment with your goals?

You can also use this method to help you overcome places where you are stuck or unclear. If you know where you want to go and plan backward, you might have sudden flashes of insight or understanding to decide how to fill in the missing piece.

One client, Elaine•, used this method to define her statistical analyses. She understood what information she wanted to end up with, and she understood with what data she was starting. Planning backward, she deconstructed the end point and was able to locate gaps in her reasoning. Once she located those gaps, she was able to consult with a couple of colleagues and could then fill in the missing pieces on her own. This, as you might imagine, gave her a sense of mastery and confidence within her process.

Sometimes, being able to combine working forward with planning backward is all you will need to overcome a dissertation obstacle.

The planning backward process works best for those graduate students who are able to keep their attention on completing the dissertation one day at a time. While you do need to have a broad picture or outline of the whole process, you can only work on whatever is in front of you today. It does little good to worry about how you'll bind the dissertation or what you'll say in your acknowledgements before you've written your first sentence. Sometimes, these daydreams can help you to keep working, and, if you use them for motivation, that's great. However, you can get caught up in all these errands and thoughts and stop making progress on the work that is in front of you right now. Aim to start each work session asking by yourself, "What is the most important thing to accomplish today?" and to end each session by asking yourself, "What was the most important thing I accomplished today?" If you like, write the answer down in your success journal. By staying tuned into the work one day at a time, you can maximize the probability that you're keeping your focus exactly where it needs to be.

Don't let the gremlins get control of the truck

Sometimes during the dissertation process, you'll be going along fine when all of a sudden, your motivation declines and your actions diminish.

Every time your motivation dips and action stalls, it's because the gremlins-those negative, whining, critical voices we carry around-have gained control of the truck. When the gremlins are in control, we begin to wonder if we'll succeed. We worry that we might be overreaching ourselves or that others will be upset by our actions. The gremlins have only one purpose: to keep you safe and small. You never have to worry about playing in the big game when the gremlins are in control.

Very often, the gremlins show up when we're tired or when we've just obtained negative feedback from our adviser or when we spend too much time in isolation and not enough time with people who love us.

Are there times in your dissertation process that you've been moving toward your goal of obtaining the Ph.D. when, all of a sudden, it seems like your progress comes to a screeching halt? Sometimes, this might be necessary; you might be waiting for some more information, a new book, or a new resource. But other times, doesn't the "stall out" happen because you've begun to doubt your idea and whether you have the intelligence, skills, or ability to create what you dream of?

It happens to all of us at one time or another. When you feel like you're like a truck that is stuck in neutral-not really moving forward but not sliding back-it's time to take a look into the driver's seat and see who's gotten control of the steering wheel. If it's a little green guy with big eyes; big teeth; and a loud, critical, nagging voice-tell him to get out of the car and catch a bus to nowhere with a one-way ticket.

By noticing the gremlins and actively working to send them away, you will attain greater inner calmness and peace. Keep focused on appropriately controlling your negative thoughts and keep moving in the direction of completing your dissertation. You can do this, and remember: the Ph.D. you want also wants you.

Time management and task planning

I recommend you consider the concept of chunking, where you take large sections and break them into smaller pieces. This can be applied to reading ("I'll read five pages and then take a break"), organizing ("I'll sort ten articles and then do something else"), or writing ("In this first thirty minutes, I will answer this question and complete this first section"). The goal in chunking is that to help you stop thinking of the dissertation process as one large piece of work and to instead see it as a wall made of bricks. Each brick represents one chunk of the wall. This can be helpful when you feel like you can't find a way into the work. Think of the work as a brick wall, and ask yourself, "What's one brick I could pull out of this wall and start working on?" This type of questioning can decrease, if not eliminate, the confusion of knowing how and where to begin. It doesn't usually matter where you start, as long as you begin.

Defining the work into chunks can be helpful in setting goals along the way. You can plan to work toward significant dates or time off by knowing how many chunks you need to complete between today and the deadline. Chunking is an effective means of dividing the dissertation process into manageable pieces.

As I've mentioned already, you want to try and avoid excess of any kind in the dissertation process. Avoid binge writing in particular. For those who don't know, binge writing is the process of not writing anything for days or weeks, and then writing furiously to meet a deadline. Then, after missing (or even meeting) the deadline, you don't write anything again for days and days. This is an extremely difficult approach toward working on the dissertation. You might have periods of binge writing in the process, perhaps when you make a new connection or figure out the solution to a complex issue. However, for the most part, most writers agree that writing every day is the best method for finishing anything. Most people cannot accomplish as much in one binge writing session once a week as they can in frequent, shorter sessions several times per week. Remember, slow and steady consistency is the fastest road to destination Ph.D.

Consistency is key aspect of goal setting. You want to set dissertation goals as you might set fitness goals. In fitness, you don't just work out once in a month and expect to see any noticeable difference. You must regularly put time in at the gym to see the results you desire. The same goes for the dissertation. You might work out for days before seeing progress but one day, you wake up and your progress is evident. If you think of the dissertation process as being like a large bottle full of sand, you will not see any change with the removal of five grains of sand from that bottle. But keep removing five 5 grains each day and, after a month, you'll see some changes in the height of the sand remaining in the bottle. On the first day, there will be no visible difference. By day 100, the change will be noticeable.

One question that comes up quite often is "How slow is too slow?" This question generally comes during the writing phase. Some students labor for days and days to write one paragraph. This is too slow. Instead, aim to write about a half page a day. If you can keep to this goal, no matter how long it takes you, you will have written about half a chapter in a month. If you keep this up for two months, you will have completed a chapter. If you are actively writing but are not reaching the one chapter mark for every six to eight weeks spent writing, it is time to seek out advice or assistance to help the process move along more quickly.

If you miss a day, try to make up the work the next day. In writing this book, my goal was to finish writing in a certain number of days. If I missed a day, I made myself make up the writing on the next day, which acted as a great incentive to keep me from missing too many days in the first place.

Another technique that might aid you in time management is to break down your tasks into five- to ten-minute intervals. Aim to accomplish three tasks at a time, and then take a break. If you routinely get sidetracked by checking e-mail or surfing the Internet, make a deal with yourself that you will work on three ten-minute tasks, and then you'll allow yourself some time for these other activities. This is a contingency type of arrangement. One woman met her goal of exercising daily by not allowing herself a shower unless she'd exercised that day. For her, the exercise was a contingency for the shower. This approach works best for those people who are disciplined enough to deny themselves e-mail or a shower if they work first. This system may not work for everyone.

Learn to say No, and use it as a time management strategy.

During the course of the dissertation process, which can take a year or more (but hopefully not too much more), you will likely be asked to help out with various events, opportunities, or committees sponsored by your academic institution, your religious institution, or your child's school.

"No, thanks" is generally tough for most people to say, especially when asked directly to participate or contribute. It's much easier to say it in a group setting or at a networking event. It seems more cutting, more personal when someone has approached you one to one, and is waiting for your answer.

Most people say agree to take on responsibilities they really don't want. Wouldn't it, just maybe, be better to say no to something you don't want to do so you can say yes to something you do?

Do you believe you have a right to life, liberty, and pursuit of happiness? Do you exercise your right to say no when you don't feel like doing something? Or, like most people, do you "yes" a bit more than you would like?

What moves you to say yes when you really don't want to? Most often, you say yes because you want to keep other people from feeling upset or hurt. You don't want them to feel angry with or disappointed in you. Maybe you fear being judged or criticized, so you say what you think they want to hear. The challenge with this approach is that people start to expect you to say yes all the time, and no becomes even more difficult to say later on.

Take a minute and think about your life. What are the situations in which you have sacrificed your personal dreams, desires, or preferences by saying yes when you really wanted to say no?

Are any of these situations occurring right now?

While I do understand that sometimes we might have to agree to do something to please someone important to us, I think it's just as important sometimes to say no to please yourself.

If you're ready to begin shifting the balance more to your favor, start small. Practice saying yes to your dreams and your desires. Think how the whole world will benefit joyfully after you do.

Learning to say no can suddenly free up a lot more time, which you can devote to accomplishing your dissertation goal much more quickly.

Finally, the best time management system is one that works for you. By noticing your own personal rhythms and honoring them, you will easily and naturally, find your own way of managing your time based on your greatest priorities. If the dissertation is a priority for you (and I'm presuming it is, since you're reading this book), then you will need to factor it into your planning for your life. I often say to my clients, "You don't probably put in your day planner a time to take a shower or a time to brush your teeth." Hopefully, you do each of these activities on automatic pilot because they are important to you and your health. If you can place the same priority on the dissertation, you will find that you have enough time to accomplish what you want to achieve. But if you say the dissertation is a priority and then avoid it and find reasons to distract yourself from it, no number of time management strategies will help you.

How do you know when you're ready to really make progress on the dissertation?

So far, you have read about a great many tools and strategies to get you working and moving ahead. This is a good time to check the areas you've worked on so far:

Self Care

Have you implemented a self care process? Are you actively working this process? Are you feeling generally good most of the time or do you remain overwhelmingly stressed out? Have you taken time to get clear on why you're doing the dissertation in the first place? Have you put some structures in place that will assist you in keeping your energy and motivation high?

Relationships

Have you structured at least two sets of support systems, one academic and one personal? Have you taken the time to explain your goals to the important people in your life, and have you been able to decrease your responsibilities so that you can focus more fully on the dissertation?

Thinking

Have you found a way to free yourself from the paralysis of negative thinking? Are you feeling reasonably hopeful and optimistic about your ability to complete this project in a timely fashion?

Work Space

Have you created a good working space for yourself? Do you have all the tools you need, and are you able to locate all your materials easily? Did you take the time to organize your articles? Is your work space both functional and appealing to you?

Work Habits

Have you set aside time to work consistently on the dissertation? Are you creating ways to pace yourself? Are you rewarding yourself along the way?

Goals

Have you taken some time to set SMART goals, one day at a time? Are you working on the dissertation consistently? Are you moving along at an adequate pace to complete about one chapter every two months?

Perfectionism

On the road of speedy dissertation progress, one of the most significant stumbling blocks is that of perfectionism. Perfectionism, in this context, means, essentially, that you are struggling with feeling that anything you write is not good enough, and so you end up spending a lot of time and energy and effort going over the same pieces over and over again.

Perfectionism can also show up in unrealistic expectations of yourself (as in "I should be able to write this right now") and of the process ("This is supposed to be moving faster than it is"). It can also show up in waiting to find the perfect time to write (which never seems to show up) and in a rigidity that the process must occur a certain way.

One client, Melissa*, was feeling unmotivated and very stuck. She began each work session by reviewing what she wrote the day before and then checking it for accuracy and proper form. She would, inevitably, find sentences that could be improved and then spend hours each day revising what she had written the day before. She came to coaching complaining of no forward progress, and no wonder. She was experiencing perfectionism and demonstrating a rigid approach to starting her work each day. In coaching, we discussed how she could start writing new material without reviewing what she had previously written as a way of short-circuiting a process that wasn't working for her. She resisted this for several days until she realized that she was putting in more than ten hours per week on the dissertation, but that most of this work had gone into just four pages. At that rate of production, she was setting herself up for five years or more of being ABD. Once we were able to identify other strategies for getting started in the work, Melissa was able to get back on track and moved somewhat more quickly from there.

In Melissa's case, she was experiencing perfectionism in several forms. She was writing too slowly, she was overed-

*Name has been changed.

iting drafts, and she was having difficulty in deciding when something was finished. As a result of her work style, she experienced extremely harsh and negative internal dialogue, which blended with her anxiety and created a very unpleasant experience.

If you are finding that you are writing too slowly, spending inordinate amounts of time on editing and reviewing what you've previously written, and putting in the time but not seeing the progress, you are likely being perfectionistic in your approach to the dissertation.

Here are some coaching tips to help you decrease your level of perfectionism in the dissertation process:

•Work in different locations. Try reading out in the sun, or revising while at a coffee shop, or doing some writing while sitting in the library. By periodically changing your work environment, you keep yourself from getting caught up in rigid, unyielding, and painful routines. The more creative you can be about finding places to work, the less likely you are to experience the rigidity and lack of innovation that often accompanies perfectionism.

•Make a pact with yourself not to edit before you write. Start each working session by writing fresh material. Write as much as you can, and then use any time left over to edit. This works to diminish perfectionism, because if you have written new material today, you are much less likely to go back and change yesterday's material. But in the absence of new writing, you may work and rework existing material and never get on to anything new.

•Remember, it's called a first draft for a reason. It is always better to draft as much of the dissertation as quickly as possible and save the editing for later. Give yourself the permission to write a poor first draft, knowing that it will improve in subsequent iterations.

• Aim to write at least one page per day, or five pages per week. If you can adhere to this guideline, no matter how difficult, you will be able to finish a dissertation chapter approximately every two months. Adhere to the guideline for now and think less about the quality of what you're writing. Much of it will improve just by the benefit of time.

• Start each working session having a clear idea of where you want to be by its end. Set SMART goals and define your aim. Once you have reached that goal, stop writing. If you aren't sure whether something is necessary to include, try leaving it out. Your adviser or committee will let you know if it's necessary. Do your best to avoid being derailed by tangents and keep asking yourself, "Is this the next most important topic to be working on?"

• Try simplifying your life. Burnout and exhaustion are other indicators of perfectionism and may indicate that you're trying to do too many things too well. If you constantly feel that you're running to stand still, some significant changes may be required in your responsibilities.

• Laugh. It's almost impossible to be perfectionistic while you're laughing. If you are feeling completely stuck, anxious, unmotivated, and like you're stuck in the same groove, do something that makes you laugh. Keep some comedies handy, or favorite comic strips, or TV shows that you can use whenever you need to laugh. This can disrupt the cycle of perfectionism and help you get back to work with a new perspective.

Procrastination

Closely tied to the concept of perfectionism is the behavior of procrastination. Most of us procrastinate when we feel a task will be too difficult for us to achieve. Sometimes, we believe that tasks are more difficult than they are, because they must be completed perfectly. The cycles of perfectionism and procrastination are tightly linked. Many graduate students feel an almost continual tension between these two experiences-if they take too long to write, then what they produce must be stunningly spectacular. If they can't produce something that stunning on the first try, they shouldn't try writing anything until they can. In this way, the movement between perfectionism and procrastination becomes a continuous loop, which leaves the ABD in the middle, feeling exhausted, unproductive, and avoidant.

It is better to set small, achievable goals. Tasks that are too difficult will lead to procrastination and avoidance. More difficult tasks are not more meaningful. In fact, what I'd love to see is more of a focus on getting the work completed rather than worrying about whether the work is stunning. The pressure to complete a stunning project is too often dealt with by avoiding the project altogether. Wouldn't it be much easier (and, maybe even fun?) to challenge yourself to complete the dissertation as easily as possible?

What if you made your own "Dissertation Game," complete with a board and pieces? For each "win," you'd get to advance your playing piece, and for every milestone, you'd gain some benefit. I'm thinking, I guess, of the Dissertation Game as being somewhat of a cross between the Life and Monopoly board games. What if you made it your mission to get around the board and to the end point as smoothly and easily as possible? By orienting yourself from the beginning to the easiest ways to accomplish your tasks, you are more likely to complete the dissertation in a timely fashion.

What's the payoff?

Do you know the main reason people don't reach their goals? It's because the emotional payoff of reaching the goal is not big enough to justify all the work. If we extend this one step further, this means that most people set goals that are too small and definitely not all that compelling.

For example, one of my clients, Maria*, came to coaching with a goal of finishing the final two chapters of her dissertation. She was excited by the benefits of doing so-she had obtained an exciting fellowship for the fall and was looking forward to finishing up before summer and taking a few months off. She also wanted to make a strong showing on the academic job market. What wasn't quite right was that she wanted all these outcomes, but was doing very little to attain them. At first, she presented the situation as if she didn't know how to finish her dissertation. Over time, it became obvious that she did know what to do, but she wasn't doing it.

After pointing out the gap between what she said she wanted-to complete the dissertation-and what she was doing-very little consistent action-we began to explore her payoff for not reaching her goals. Maria's payoffs included: 1) avoiding discomfort, because she didn't want to struggle with some unfinished ideas in her next chapter; 2) holding on to her limiting beliefs, because she had some small, niggling doubts about her skills and didn't want others to find out; and 3) fear, because she didn't want to finish up and find that she wasn't a strong candidate for an academic job.

*Name has been changed.

As you can see, the payoff for inaction was quite high. She wouldn't have to put herself out there or be uncomfortable, nor would she have to face the fear that she might not be as good as she thought, nor would she have to find a way to balance her fear with her achievements.

Once these hidden payoffs became evident, Maria was able to look at them more clearly and directly- and she realized that some of them were silly reasons not to take action. She was able to see that having a completed dissertation in hand would help her be more successful in all areas of her life: she'd have more time for her husband, and she could enjoy some hobbies and activities, and she could feel more confident interviewing for jobs.

In grasping her hidden payoffs for inaction, Maria was then able to choose a new course of action. She moved into high gear, and got busy with writing and counting down to the finish line.

As Einstein once said, "Nothing happens until something moves." If you're feeling frozen and unable to move forward toward achieving your goals, look for the hidden payoff in staying right where you are. This, very often, will help you start to move forward once again.

Once you've decided that the hidden payoffs aren't worth it, here are some steps to assist you in breaking through procrastination:

• Do the worst things first. Have a task that you absolutely can't stand? Try working on it first. Get it out of your way so you can stop worrying about it.

• Can't figure it out? Get help. If you are procrastinating, it's a fair guess that you probably don't know what you need to do next. It is rare that people procrastinate when they have a compelling argument or have worked out all the details of what they want to write. If you can't figure it out, talk it over with someone on your support team so you can get a new perspective and new clarity.

•Monitor your self care. Sometimes, we procrastinate more when we've pushed ourselves to work very hard without a break. Our mind and body start to rebel over time, and want to only focus on meaningless tasks like playing computer games. When this happens, it's a good time to take a break and do what you can to recharge and refresh. There is no point in pushing yourself to work more when you are not feeling productive.

•Ask yourself: What am I afraid of? And listen to the answer. Often, procrastination is a way of avoiding fear. If you take a few minutes and journal your answer to the question, "What am I afraid of?" That can help clear out the negative, critical voices that are keeping the procrastination firmly in place.

•Look for the easy way. Find the easiest way possible to complete the task in front of you. Ask yourself, "Since I have to do this, what would be the easiest and most pleasant way to complete this?" and then listen for the answer. Find that little bit of relief in that tiny feeling of "Ohh, that would make it better" and then make whatever changes you need to complete the task as easily as possible.

Researching

Many students feel overwhelmed by the amount and complexity of research required for the dissertation. The following are some thoughts on how you can complete the research process with a less frustration and stress.

•Simple is best. It might seem paradoxical or at least counterintuitive, but the same research strategies you used to complete your elementary school research paper will often work for your dissertation process. The act of researching and writing is fairly consistent across the educational lifespan; only the topics and techniques become more complex. If you take a few minutes and think back to the research strategies you learned in elementary school, you will find useful processes for completing your dissertation.

One of the best ways to organize your notes is on three-by-five-inch index cards, just like you did in your early education. Yes, while these cards can be sometimes unwieldy or become overwhelming, they are a much, much better alternative than hundreds of notes in an electronic file that are neither organized nor easy to access. Many of my clients initially wasted a lot of time in scrolling through pages of computer screens to find notes relevant to their particular focus at that time. If you are just beginning the research process, I'd recommend that you get in the habit of jotting down notes on index cards. Create a master key that lists the article title, author, and a color coded symbol (red triangle, blue dot, etc.) so that you can easily locate the source from which the note comes. On the top left-hand corner of the card, put the symbol denoting the article from which the content comes (for example, a red triangle for article 1, a blue circle for article 2, etc.). Further down on the card, list just one idea or item of importance from the article.

After time, you will have stacks of note cards for this project. This can be overwhelming if you keep all the cards together. You will find it easier to manage your data if you chunk your note cards by chapter as we previously discussed. At any one time, you should only be actively handling cards related to the chapter on which you're currently working. You can, of course, take notes on any chapter, and the beauty of note cards is that they can be shuffled and moved until you find the best fit.

Before you write your chapter, take all the note cards for that chapter and lay them out in groups by section/topic/idea. Order the note cards into the correct sequence. Then, begin writing. Using note cards may preclude the necessity of a detailed outline, which can save you time during the writing process. Also, note cards provide a visual pathway for the way your dissertation will proceed. This structure is often helpful in providing some boundaries or a framework for your writing sessions.

If you already have pages of notes in your computer, you might want to print out a copy, mark each note with the appropriate reference symbol so you know the article from which it came, and then cut these notes into strips so that you have one idea per strip. Group these strips of notes into the correct chapters or sections and use these strips just as you would note cards. Consider using a plastic sleeve or sheet protector so you can keep all the strips together. Label this sleeve or protector with the chapter and section to which the notes relate.

By making a master key at the beginning and adding to it along the way, you also create a more complete rough draft of your bibliography. To create the master color key, you will need about five to seven colored markers or pencils. At first, the symbols will be easy to use red circle, blue circle, green circle and so on. Then you can go into triangles, squares, and stars; stick with the simplest shapes. If you start to run out of color and figure options, consider blending them: red square/blue circle for one source, two red squares for another, two blue stars for another. If needed, you can expand your range by using a three-color/symbol combination. If you find yourself getting confused, remember that you can always invest in a set of thirty colored pencils or markers to keep the keying process simpler. Just make sure you don't use colors that are too similar to each other and therefore difficult to tell apart.

Another advantage to using the note card system is that you can carry an article and a few cards with you wherever you go, and therefore take advantage of dead time. If you have read my other book, *Get it Done! A Coach's Guide to Dissertation Success!*, you know that I'm a big proponent of using all the little pockets of time you can find to create momentum for your dissertation. While you're waiting in line at the bus stop or riding the subway, you can revise a few pages or take a few notes on an article. If you are working full time, and you have a long commute by subway or train, consider using that time to do some dissertation research. Take your article, a stack of about ten to fifteen cards, and your pen-and then go to work. You can easily take notes on an article in about ten to fifteen minutes, which can give you a sense of accomplishment and more motivation to complete the dissertation.

Note cards are also a useful tool for limiting how much you write. Often, you take more notes than you need or will use, just because it's easy to type into the computer. When you are handwriting notes, you may find it easier to hone in on what you really need or will use to save the time and effort of writing too much on a card. Note cards can move you to focus in on what's truly important and provide a means for making notes and capturing information when a computer is not easily accessible.

• Use as few sources as possible to make your point. Most people during the research phase use the kitchen sink approach; they toss everything into the research just in case they find something they might need. I recommend that instead, you get clear on what the top five to seven points are for each chapter. After this, get clear on how many sources you will need to support each major point in this particular chapter. There will often be some sources you read for overview knowledge, some you read for supplementary knowledge, and some sources you actually cite in the body of your paper. A good rule of thumb, as you begin, is to find two or three overview articles and about three to five articles per main point, then limit your supplementary materials to about five to seven additional sources. Some projects may need more sources, and some will use less; use the above numbers as a rule of thumb. The reason for limiting your sources to the fewest number necessary is to keep you from inundating yourself with books, articles, and papers that you might never get to read but will certainly make you feel guilty for not reading each time you look at them. Instead, aim for a clean, spare approach. Get what you need, and not much more.

As you know, it's usually very easy to add more sources to your project; it's more difficult to prune them down. I suggest that you prune first and add later if necessary. If you have three to five respected, journal-accepted articles to support each key point that you make, that will often provide a strong enough foundation to carry the paper.

So if you are just beginning the research phase, you will want to start by obtaining your two to three overview articles and getting a sense of the current overview on the issue or issues you will be addressing. Next, you will want to search through the reference list of these articles and start finding likely sources for additional research. If, at this point, you have some idea of the points you will be discussing, look specifically for articles that reflect these points. If you aren't sure, aim to gather only about seven to ten articles for each section or chapter. If you've selected well, you should find the beginnings of the information you'll need. It's better at first to plan several shorter research trips rather than long days spent chasing down obscure articles that you might not even use.

A good research paradigm would be to spend a few hours obtaining research, to then make time to take notes on these articles and texts, and to then plan another day to go back and fill in the holes or whatever might be missing. It's good, too, to try to write the relevant sections as soon as you can; sometimes, moving in a cycle of researching, organizing, writing, researching, organizing, writing can be more effective than doing all the research at once, all the organization at once, and all the writing at once. Most graduate students respond well to a varied working routine. By splitting up the writing into smaller pieces, it feels more manageable, which is an additional bonus of using this kind of working pattern.

Another useful approach in the research phase is to try to impose as much order as possible ahead of time. Don't wait to figure out your organization and filing approach until you've brought home 100 articles. Instead, create a system ahead of time and then obtain the information needed. Whether you use a filing cabinet, three-ring binders, plastic sleeves, or some other system to organize your materials, aim to get this set up so that your research materials have a place to go right from the beginning. This will save you from having piles of paper all over your desk and from having to sort through a stack of information to find the one quote or sentence you're looking for. Visual clutter can be overwhelming and continually having to rustle through papers to find something is not an efficient way to work.

•Consider tools that might help. Again, in the spirit of completing the dissertation as easily as possible, I invite you to consider all the options you might have to make the research process easier. You might, for instance, consider using bibliographic software. You might hire an undergraduate research assistant. You might get assistance from your school's librarian, who can often find information more quickly and easily than you can. You might use interlibrary loan to save yourself a trip to a neighboring school, and you might consider using online searchable databases to narrow down your searches before even going to the library.

Aim to complete your research in a timely, efficient, and well-thought-out way. Avoid the approach where you just photocopy every item that might be remotely relevant. Instead, consider first what the aims of your research are: are you looking to gain a broad overview of the issues? To supplement what you know? Or to find certain reviewed journals to support your viewpoint? Are you looking for newest work by premier researchers in your field? Or are you looking for a topic to study in the first place? Your answers to these questions should be the shaping force in how you approach the research phase for your project.

If you are looking for a topic or want to further explore the viability of your topic, remember to check out the discussion sections of published articles (also sometimes titled "for further research" or "ideas for future consideration") and don't forget to check out the listing of dissertation abstracts. Often, you can find others who are studying your topic and get good ideas from them.

Also, part of your research process should always include a review of at least four completed dissertations from your department, preferably on a topic that is similar to yours. By reading through these successful dissertations, you will be able to understand what your finished product should resemble. Like many life experiences, with the dissertation, if you don't know where you're going, you won't know when you get there. So make sure you spend a bit of time reviewing relevant dissertations so you can see how it's done.

• Use visual/creative tools to create research questions and follow connections. During the research and writing phases of the dissertation, it's very likely that you will come to a point where you feel confused and as if you don't know how to move forward with your ideas. When this occurs, it can mean that you've recently taken in a great deal of new information but haven't yet had the opportunity to solidify and integrate your understanding of it. The resulting confusion and lack of clarity can be both anxiety provoking ("What if I never have another idea ever again?") and overwhelming ("What will I do if I can't get this finished by the deadline?"). When you are feeling anxious and overwhelmed and don't know quite how to proceed, don't just sit there-do something. Consider using Mind Mapping, brainstorming, or storyboarding to help facilitate your thinking and creative process.

Mind Mapping, developed in the 1940s by Tony Buzan, is a visual thinking tool that allows you to generate a larger number of ideas or connections between ideas. Mind Mapping requires a piece of paper and a pen or pencil. If you are more comfortable using a computer, consider obtaining one of the free programs available on the Internet. I like and use Freemind; download pages can be found by using your favorite search engine. This is how to get started:

Take your sheet of paper (or computer screen) and start by filling in the word, idea, or phrase you need to generate some ideas about. Borrowing from an earlier example, let's return back to the automobile design topic. You would take a phrase like "interior design" and put this in the center of the page. Then you'd draw lines (like the spoke of a wheel) radiating out from the words. Quickly, lightly, and easily, you'll fill in other words related to the word or phrase in the center. You might add words and phrases like: comfort, beauty, cost effective, easy to maintain. For every word you add, you'll draw more lines radiating out and fill in words from there, and so on. When you've completed the Mind Map, you'll have a series of interconnected suns or wheels that will demonstrate a detailed progression of ideas that can form the basis for an outline or give you more information about how to focus and shape your approach. Entire books have been written about this subject; a more detailed overview can be found by visiting Tony Buzan's Web site at http://www.mind-map.com.

Brainstorming is another technique that can assist you in creating connections to help you move ahead with your work. Brainstorming relies on a generation of ideas in a quick, easy, and light way. Instead of drawing the radiant lines or suns, brainstorming can occur as more of a list of ideas. For those of you who are more linear thinkers may find brainstorming a more appealing technique to try when you need more ideas. In all of these techniques, it's a good idea to keep your ideas in one place and hold on to them for future reference. You might be surprised at how often the seed of a good idea comes up in your first Mind Map or brainstorm and then how easily it can be lost or forgotten. Keep all of your notes, doodles, and ideas; these are all part of your creative process and may come in handy, as this example will attest:

Laura* had been making steady progress on the dissertation for several months. She was just about to start her final chapter when she seemed to get derailed. She found it difficult to find the central theme or structure for this chapter and began to feel anxious and worried about her inability to get going on this chapter. Her deadline was just about two months away. After a week of restless worrying, she suddenly remembered that she had worked out some ideas for this chapter several months before. She went through
*Name has been changed.

her notes from her catchall file and found some handwritten thoughts pertaining to this chapter. She quickly generated a Mind Map from these thoughts and was able to draw enough useful connections so that she could get back to writing. Once she had this breakthrough, her anxiety diminished and she was able to get back to working on her final chapter in a directed and steady way. [And yes, she did meet her deadline and defended soon after.]

The moral of the story is to keep all the scraps of paper and random notes you take through the course of dissertation process. You'll never know when one of them will provide the spark for a Mind Map or brainstorm that helps you lock your ideas into place and write on them.

Both Mind Mapping and brainstorming are good techniques for when you need to create additional associations or links between existing ideas. They can be used to expand your topic laterally, horizontally, or vertically-meaning you can make the topic broader, wider, more focused, or more distilled through your creation of a Mind Map. In contrast, however storyboarding is a technique that can help you create a logical sequence of your ideas and thoughts and is best for creating linear sequences.

To craft a storyboard, you'll need a package of three-by-four-inch sticky notes and a blank wall or bulletin board. On each sticky note, jot down one idea or one sentence that you already know or have in mind. You'll then place these notes in a linear/chronological order on the wall. Very often, you will have an idea and an end point you'd like to reach, but the steps in between will be unknown. When you know where you're starting from and you know where you'd like to go, then you start at the end and work backward. Let's say that you are working out a strong argument for this chapter. You'd start by putting a note that reads: Strong argument found at one end of your wall or bulletin board. Then you'd place a note reading, "Starting here, don't have much of an argument." Then, working backward from the end, you would start placing notes that would define the steps that need to occur before reaching the desired end point. You'd work backward until you have filled in most of the steps. You might have branches coming off the steps (for example, if you need to read an article first), but you should, after this is done, have a road map of how you will proceed.

This planning backward process can also be used to ascertain deadlines for setting goals in your dissertation process. See the chapter on goal setting for more information about this technique.

Getting down to writing

Writing the dissertation requires preparation-of both the content and the writer. You must gather your ideas together, organize them, and be able to transfer your three-dimensional intimacy with your topic to the two-dimensional framework of the computer screen or pad of paper. This is often one of the most difficult transitions to make, for you must first build up a structure and then tear it down and separate it into parts to make it fit the prescribed structure of an acceptable dissertation.

Most graduate students are synthetic thinkers; that is, they are prone to thinking about the big picture. They love to roll ideas around and find all sorts of connections and combinations and links within the seemingly limitless realm of thinking. Generally, it is neither as interesting nor as easy to transfer the unlimited potential of your thoughts to the less exciting and interesting realm of words on paper. For those of you who are at ease with writing, you might be wondering how anyone could have trouble expressing their thoughts in the written word. However, my professional experience suggests that most dissertators find the writing phase to be quite challenging.

Why is the writing phase one of the most difficult aspects of the dissertation process? I suspect that this is related to several factors:

1) Thinking is creative and generative; writing can sometimes be mechanical. When you are in the beginning of the dissertation process, you are likely to be very excited and interested in your topic. You might be meeting with other professors and colleagues to talk about your ideas, and you might be feeling excited by all the terrific thoughts you're having. By the time you get to the writing phase, you might be less excited about your topic, might be working more in isolation, and might be experiencing the writing as somewhat mechanistic. All of this can be a letdown after the enthusiasm of coming up with an idea and learning all that you can about it.

2) Some people find writing difficult. As someone who likes to write, this is hard for me to understand, but it does appear that a strong percentage of people find writing to be very challenging and hard to do. They feel like they freeze and that their thoughts don't come as easily when they have to express themselves on paper or computer screen.

3) Writing can be tedious. Sometimes, it's just a matter of stating what you already know, so there is little spark or excitement in quantifying what you've already studied.

4) Writing can be lonely. Most graduate students end up writing in solitude, whether they like it or not. It can be difficult to be isolated and working on a project such as this, so some ABDs avoid writing in order to avoid experiencing the anxiety or isolation that can be part of the writing phase.

5) Writing often requires a well-developed capacity for delayed gratification. Now, by the time you've been in school for so many years, you are likely to feel that you're an expert in delaying gratification. After all, how much have you delayed and sacrificed to make it to this point? However, writing the dissertation can stretch you further than you've gone before. While you desire to complete the

project, there will be days when you wonder if you have what it takes to keep putting your life on hold while you work on this project. Now, while occasional sacrifices might be necessary, remember that in the long term, there are no extra points for ongoing suffering.

When you are preparing to write a chapter or section of the dissertation, there are certain processes that can make it easier to begin and keep working:

First, follow your own natural style of organizing information, within reason. Your usual style of reading, studying, and integrating information has served you well up to this point in your academic career. Now, in the home stretch, is not the time to radically change your organizing and writing style. Use what works for you and stay focused on completing this project as quickly as possible. Some graduate students view the dissertation as the time to rid themselves of all their bad work habits so they can finally reach the exalted place they've always aspired to be. Allow me to suggest that you save the self-exaltation for after you obtain your Ph.D. There will be plenty of time in your post-Ph.D. life to become the super sophisticated and rigorous scholar you desire to be. Until you have been awarded your degree, stay with what has worked well for you. If you read best in bed at night, by all means keep doing that. If you write best first thing in the morning, keep doing that. If you like to have the radio on while you're piecing out a complex train of thought, leave it on. The dissertation is the time to keep on using what has worked for you so far. It's not the time to try to change yourself drastically.

Some of the tips in this book will be extensions of your natural style; others you may gravitate toward after trial and you may desire to adopt these more fully. If any of the suggestions in this book are completely antithetical to how you work, see if you can find a way to keep the spirit of the advice without retaining the structure. If you have no existing structure for certain tasks, start by borrowing some of the ideas provided here. If you come up with a better adaptation or a unique twist that serves you well, by all means implement its. While the end point of the dissertation is well defined, the process generally varies by individual.

In preparing to write, it is a good idea to take some time to review your notes and what you are planning to say. I suggest doing this for about fifteen to twenty minutes before your official writing time. If you work in the morning, for example, you might sit at your desk at 8:35 a.m. and read over your notes until 9 a.m. Then you'd start your official writing time, which might last until 9:30 a.m. After this, you might take a break for a few minutes, walk around, stretch, and then precede your next writing burst with a brief period of reading and reflection. When you are first sitting down to write, schedule shorter writing periods (especially if you find writing to be difficult) and gradually work up from there.

Remember, as we've already touched on, more hours spent in front of the computer do not automatically make the finished product better. If you can get a focused block of writing time and use it well, you can accomplish a great deal in smaller blocks of writing time, even fifteen to thirty minutes. The longer you sit at the computer without writing, the more likely it is that your internal critic is censoring you, and the more your critic censors you, the more difficult you'll find it to write. So if you're having problems finding the right words or nothing is coming out, shift your focus for a few minutes and then try again. There is nothing to be gained in focusing on how you should be writing something when you're not.

Focus is a significant aspect of preparing to write. Stay focused on the section or chapter you're working on, and try not to get derailed by too many thoughts about random ideas. Having too many good ideas about the parts of the dissertation you're not currently working on can be an avoidance technique. You might want to keep a note pad by your computer so you can jot down your ideas and file them away for use later. Unless you are absolutely compelled to switch focus and move to a new topic or section, try to adhere to your original plan. Inspiration does strike, and should be welcomed. But overall, the main progress of the dissertation will often be more plodding and methodical.

Make use of your visual aids to assist in writing. If you made a Mind Map or outline of this section, go back and fill in as many details as possible. Refer to this map or outline periodically and aim to end each writing session by reaching a defined goal. The clearer you are about where you're going, the easier it will be to know when you've reached there.

Steve Manning (http://www.writeabooknow.com) suggests that you write a detailed outline for every section and shape each comment in the form of a question to be answered. So, instead of writing: "Comment on the exterior design of automobiles in the 1920s," you'd write: "What were the common factors in exterior automobile design in the 1920s?" By writing each topic in the form of a question, Manning states that it will be easier to write the answers, which will become the text for that chapter or section. Manning also suggests that, if you're stuck on what to write, that you make sure you address the main questions of who, what, why, where, when, and how, then number the answers in a linear or chronological sequence so the writing flows logically.

It's crucial that you've attended to any negative feelings and gotten them out of your way before sitting down to write. If you are feeling tired, depressed, angry, anxious, or upset-do something to alleviate these feelings first so you can then have a more successful writing experience. One technique that I use quite often is to write a journal entry for about ten to fifteen minutes before starting to write. I find that this helps me dump out all my thoughts, worries, and mental wanderings, clearing my mind so there is space to focus on the writing task at hand.

If you find that you're sitting in front of the computer and aren't sure what to say, try opening a blank document and jotting down what you're thinking and feeling. If you don't know what to say, start by saying "I don't know what to say." Write about what you want to accomplish in this writing burst, and what you think will help you accomplish your goal. This type of free writing can often prime the pump and get the ideas flowing more smoothly.

Also, as you prepare to write, try starting with the section or idea with which you feel most comfortable. In every writing session, aim to draft at least half a page, no matter how terrible that half page might be. There is value in writing for the sake of writing, especially at first, and you might create nuggets that can be expanded in later sections.

I also recommend that you allow yourself to sink into the writing and sometimes allow your intuition a freer rein. I find that when I get into the writing zone, the words keep coming out of me and they flow easily. When I start to edit and revise in mid-sentence, the writing zone quickly disappears and is difficult to find again. I must stress that when you are writing, write! Aim to write as much as you can as fast as you can. When you are editing, edit! Do this carefully and thoughtfully. You will know the difference because the writing will flow more easily and you will be almost continuously typing when you are writing, just writing. When you are editing your writing as you write it, your time at the computer or desk will be marked by long pauses; little output; and a growing feeling of anxiety, worry, and, sometimes even dread.

Remember: you cannot write quickly and edit at the same time. Writing and editing should be considered to be mutually exclusive for your purposes. Create a psychological or emotional writing space that allows you to explore your ideas without feeling they always have to lead to perfect, well-defined end points. If you have read enough and prepared an outline or map for your writing, sometimes you just need to step aside and allow the writing to come. The writing is not going to show up when your internal critic is judging every word you type. Writing is a creative process, and creation is often messy. The more you can allow the writing to be messy, the faster you will move to the place of a more refined product.

Consistency and routine will aid you in your writing process. The more you can create systems and rituals that gently prepare you to begin writing, the easier it will be to slip into the writing and move ahead with it. If possible, try to work at the same time every day and for the same amount of time every day. This should be focused writing time.

Aim to create a working process that allows you to prepare before sitting down to write. Whether you read your notes the night before or just a few minutes before writing, create clear divisions between the kinds of work you're doing. You will not find a flow of words coming out of you if you keep stopping every few seconds to look up a note or figure out how to cite an author's name. It's better to mark these places with capital letters like (BBB or CCC or ZZZ) or with brackets or highlight marks and come back and fill them in later. If you want to create momentum in your writing, aim to get yourself into a cycle of preparing to write, writing, preparing to write, and then writing again. Save editing and revising for those days where you might not have time or energy to write or for those days when your ideas are still coalescing and the writing is not coming together as smoothly as usual.

As I mentioned earlier, it works well to leave your last sentence unfinished so you can more easily pick up in mid-thought when you next return to writing. Most ABDs find it much more daunting to start on a new page or with a new paragraph compared to finishing up one they had already been working on. Each time you sit down to write, aim to work for at least ten to fifteen minutes at a time. If you think this doesn't sound like much time, you're right. But if you write for the whole ten to fifteen minutes, you can easily write a page or more within that time frame. Then you can go out and do other things. Remember, the dissertation is just a long paper. The more you can chip away at it by writing a little each day, the sooner you will get to the finish line.

Another important phase of writing is to be able to work in a quiet and (shall I say?) boring space with few distractions. If you are prone to checking e-mail or surfing the Internet, work on a computer that does not allow ready access to these distractions. As has been previously mentioned, author Susan Perry interviewed many writers- all of whom basically said that they work in the most boring rooms of their houses. Most authors interviewed tended to favor small spaces with very little in the way of views. One author, in fact, was quoted as saying that the view outside his window was so boring that he couldn't do anything but write. Within reason, this is what you want to create. Note, please, though, that spare doesn't mean uncomfortable. You don't have to suffer to get this done. You just need to focus on it for about twenty minutes per day, at least five days per week. It sounds deceptively simple, but you'd be surprised at how few graduate students really demonstrate this kind of commitment and discipline to the process. More often, they are thinking about how they're not working on their dissertation, when they could actually be working on it and making definable progress in just twenty minutes per day.

The antidote to this, of course, is to think less and do more. Rather than taking up all the valuable real estate in your very expensive brain by charting out the perfect pathway to a perfect dissertation that may never get written, why not do a bit more and think a bit less? When you're writing the

117

dissertation, your main goal should be to fill as many pages with as good quality writing as you can, as quickly as you can. If you can't write fast and well, then at least write fast. Writing fast often turns out better than we expect, anyway. If you have taken the steps to outline your thoughts and you have read enough in the topic, the only goal you should have is to get as much of your knowledge out onto the screen or paper as quickly as you can.

Remember, the dissertation is not a masterpiece in the first draft. And it's not a work of pure fiction (we hope), so you don't have to worry about snazzy plot lines, intriguing climaxes, or the ideal amount of tension between your characters. Since the dissertation is a formal piece of academic writing, you will need to follow the style and form of this genre, and this rarely requires the amount of pre-thought that most ABDs put into it. The first chapters of the dissertation are the most difficult to write because you are becoming accustomed to a more formal, scholarly style of writing. Once you have the basic format defined, you will want to use a similar template for each of your subsequent chapters. Again, the work needn't be painful to be meaningful.

To get a sense of the order and flow of a dissertation, it is wise to read a few dissertations from your department so you can develop an organic sense of how the paper flows. Notice how the paper is laid out, notice how citations are handled, notice how many articles are referenced for each major point. If you can, try to construct a working template to use as a rough guide for your own work. Note how long each chapter is, see how the author treated direct quotes, and notice how the footnotes were handled. Your mission is to make your paper match as closely as possible to those dissertations that have already been approved by your department. Pay attention to grammar, word choice, verb tense, and syntax. Once you have taken the time to read through three or four completed papers, you will have a more complete understanding of how to structure your paper so that it is acceptable to your adviser and committee.

The dissertation process is a well-trod path in some ways; you needn't be highly innovative in the process of completing it. It's not necessarily exciting or dynamic, but more an opportunity to show that you can capably step into the role of academia as it's been defined and handed down. Your writing will be original, but the underlying framework of each dissertation is basically the same.

If you have spent a lot of time thinking and have little output to show for it, I'll request, right now, that you aim to think less and do more. It doesn't matter how great the dissertation is in your head; if it's not out on paper, it doesn't count.

Set realistic deadlines

In the writing phase, be sure to keep your motivation alive by setting realistic deadlines. A deadline is realistic, for you if your reaction to it is, "Oh, I can easily do that, no sweat." Remember, you can always beat a deadline you've set. Most often, though, ABDs set deadlines that are so grand there is no way they will ever be met, which leads to a cycle of feeling like a failure, working feverishly, and then getting derailed and finding it difficult to get started or moving ahead again. Find a better way.

If you get stuck in the writing and are finding it difficult to move forward, you might try talking out loud about your ideas and how they might fit together. Hearing yourself talk can sometimes break down a block and get you back to writing. Another idea would be to talk out loud and tape yourself and then transcribe the tape. This can give you some words on paper, forming the first rough draft and helping you get started. Also, if you have trusted colleagues or a writing group, you can try talking with them about your writing. Feeling supported can go a long way in preparing to write.

Finally, once you find a routine that works, make a conscious and deliberate attempt to use it each day. Keep track of what feels best to you as you work; the more your working time feels pleasant and useful, the more you will be reinforced to work.

Remember to use visual aids to track your progress. One client used a map of the United States of America and took himself on a "walking tour" of America-for every hour worked, he moved a straight pin about sixty miles farther on a highway. By the time defended, he'd already "visited" Las Vegas, Orlando, Minneapolis, and New York City (twice!) and he had a lot of fun completing the writing. Incidentally, he also saved up for a trip to see some of these places in person after defending. By having fun with the process, he made the writing phase much easier on himself and found himself actually looking forward to working.

Also, during the writing phase, set up (and keep) regular contact with your adviser so you don't feel awkward or overwhelmed when it is time to meet with him or her. Staying in touch need not be an elaborate affair; it can be as simple as a monthly e-mail saying, "Hi, hope you're well, I'm still working. Will send more product soon" or something similar. This keeps your adviser in the loop and can keep the process moving more smoothly. Plus, it can increase your motivation to write, since you know that someone is waiting on the other end to read it.

Intrapersonal /interpersonal issues

There are several kinds of intrapersonal and interpersonal issues that can negatively impact your rate and type of dissertation progress. Among these are isolation, a reluctance to ask for help, unresolved disagreements or conflicts with your adviser or peers, difficulties moving on from rejection, a lack of mentoring and collegial relationships, and personal/intimate relationship problems. Let's discuss each in more detail.

Isolation can become a problem in several ways during the dissertation process. It can be isolating for the ABD who makes the shift from attending classes and seminars regularly to working alone on the dissertation. It can feel both jarring and abrupt to move from the camaraderie of preparing for comprehensive exams to the solitude of researching and writing a dissertation. Isolation can also become more pronounced for those graduate students who are studying areas that are not well supported in their academic departments. These students experience a special burden of isolation because they are moving out into a world that is not well populated with advisers/mentors from their own fields of expertise and experience. Isolation can, then, be of the physical, intellectual, or emotional variety-and sometimes, all three at once.

Another type of isolation is experienced when a graduate student moves away from his/her home university during the dissertation year. Quite often, these moves are for personal reasons. In these situations, the graduate student becomes both physically and geographically isolated. Even though e-mail and voice mail can help bridge the distance, these are rarely complete substitutes for the "in the flesh" human interactions that were easy to find when you lived just a few minutes from campus. Students who move to new geographical locations during the dissertation year must plan for a period of disruption and internal disarray as they settle into their new living environments.

A third type of isolation seems to happen between dissertators and their junior peers. Sometimes, working on the dissertation can leave you feeling "out of sight, out of mind," and you might need to work a bit harder to get the time, interest, and effort of your junior peers and advisers. It's not fair, to be sure, but there is often the sense that by the time someone has begun work on the dissertation, s/he is on the way out and therefore could not possibly require the same level of time, interest, and participation as before. This is incorrect. It might be that dissertators actually need more time, interest, and participation from key people since they are venturing out into a new academic and professional realm.

The fourth type of isolation is that of being the only person you know who is working on a dissertation. This tends to arise more frequently in those students who move away from campus or who have significant personal commitments outside of graduate school. These students may find that the dissertation almost continually impedes their capacity to take part in other activities and, after time, they may begin to feel isolated and resentful about the demands of this project. They start to question if completing this project is worth it, and they struggle to balance all the activities in their lives.

No matter what type of isolation you might be experiencing, the solution is the same: connect with more like-mind-ed people. It might feel overwhelming (oh no! one more thing to do) but the benefits will far outweigh the time spent searching for these people. If you are isolated and still near campus, try to find others who are in your same circumstance. Consider starting a writer's group or a working team where you meet with each other, but then spend the time together working individually on your projects. It's the equivalent of working "with" someone, even though you are working on different things.

If you have moved away from campus and are feeling isolated, consider meeting other dissertators through coffee shops, trips to the local educational library, free ads in the local paper, or fliers posted on community bulletin boards. Try to reach out to others in your new community who might be working on the same kinds of things; you will gain both academic and personal support by doing so. Also, stay in touch with your colleagues and peers at your home institution and plan trips to go back every few months, coinciding, if at all possible, with major milestones in your dissertation process.

If you want to stay connected to your peers and friends in graduate school, make a concerted effort to keep in touch. Join your school's e-mail list, offer to help junior peers navigate the comprehensive or orals exam process, and share your progress and dissertation/life updates. Aim to be both interested and interesting.

When you are the only one in your peer group who is working on a dissertation, be prepared for the strong possibility that others just won't understand. You will need to set boundaries around your time, energy, and responsibilities so you can complete this project. If your friends want to assist you, let them. Tell them what to look for in your qualitative data, get some help with data entry, ask them to type up your bibliography, or let them help you file and organize your office. By allowing others to take part in your work, no matter how small or seemingly insignificant their contribution, the more likely it is that you will feel supported in your work, which will diminish your feelings of isolation and resentment.

The Internet should not be overlooked as a viable option for meeting other dissertators. There are several online groups in which dissertators support each other. For parents, there are the ABD Moms and ABD Dads group. These are online email based lists where participants can post suggestions and ask for support. They are free of charge and require only internet access. In order to subscribe to these lists, you'll need to send a blank email to ABDMoms-subscribe@yahoogroups.com for the ABD Moms list or to a blank email to ABDDads-subscribe@yahoogroups.com for the ABD Dads list. You might also find other groups by using Internet search engines. Or, start your own group and create support that way.

Reluctance to Ask for Help

One of the most significant factors of dissertation delay (which often leads to dissertation derailment) is the graduate student's reluctance or ambivalence in asking for help. Somewhere in the years of academia, it has become more noble and valuable to suffer in silence rather than seek out the help you need to finish. How many ABDs waste months and years of their lives trying to figure out the answer to something and just not getting it? How many ABDs would be better served by asking for help and learning how to find the answer they are seeking?

Create a Helper's List.

At minimum, you should already have contacts with various people who can help you with various tasks. Consider creating a helper's list. For example, you should have someone you can ask for help with statistics or qualitative research. You should have someone who can critique your writing (and this could be a trusted friend, peer, or relative). You should have some friends to whom you can complain. You should have an adviser who can at least provide the basic information you need to move ahead. Try to develop a good working relationship with your department's support staff, as they can be invaluable, especially when you are working off campus or away from the university. Have a computer support or technical person who can help you with any computer or technology glitches. Make friends with your reference librarian, as s/he can assist you in locating obscure texts or other research materials. If you are prone to isolating yourself under stress, consider having a loosely organized dissertation writing group to keep you on track. Finally, if you feel that professional assistance might serve you, keep handy the numbers for a therapist or coach who can guide you over any rough spots.

It's a good idea, also, to have all the technical support phone numbers and key contacts for any kind of hardware or software you might be using in the dissertation process. This information can come in handy if the night before you're turning in your completed paper, you can't figure out how to properly paginate the entire document. Gather names and assistance everywhere you can.

If you have children, your helper's list may include the names and contact information for sitters and day care facilities. You might have the names of restaurants and grocery stores that deliver. You never really know at the start what kind of help you'll need by the end, so update your helper's list regularly.

A side benefit of the helper's list is that just looking at it can remind you that you're not alone and that you do, in fact, have many resources and forms of help available-if you ask.

There are no extra points for going the dissertation distance without help. At minimum, the process can be tedious, isolating, and difficult. The more support you ask for and accept, the easier and more quickly the process can move.

It's always better to ask for help than to suffer in silence.

Unresolved Conflicts With Advisers and Peers

Another area that needs to be looked at is that of unresolved conflicts with your adviser and/or peers. Too often, ABDs feel negative about themselves and their work, and this can be directly linked to criticism offered by a key academic person in the ABD's experience. While constructive criticism is necessary to guide your project to completion, too often ABDs are given conflicting or competing information and have difficult in knowing how to reconcile it. The task begins to feel overwhelming and progress stops.

When working with my coaching clients who have suddenly stopped progressing, we always start by looking at the circumstances surrounding the derailment. In more than 90 percent of the cases, the derailment can be directly related to a negative comment or a feeling of frustration/conflict with an adviser or a peer. Many times, ABDs don't even recognize that they are reacting to this event, and so the derailment feels mysterious and unexplainable. If you have ever felt your motivation for this project suddenly dip or disappear for some amount of time, try thinking back to the events leading up to this change. My guess is that you felt criticized or in conflict related to your work.

Since expressing your feelings is one of the best ways to get over them, your next task is to find a safe place and a safe person (or two) with whom you can share your feelings. You want to find someone who you know is trustworthy and who supports and understands you. Sometimes, another academician is a good option as s/he has probably experienced some of the same types of events and may have some helpful insights. The possible downside to this approach, though, is that academia is quite competitive, and should you select someone in your department, you might find that s/he ends up using information against you. I'd recommend that you always seek support and assistance outside of your department first, so you have a clear boundary between what you share and how it can be used in the future.

If, however, your conflict is with your adviser, you might not be able to talk it out with anyone except him or her. If you plan to speak with your adviser, here are some ideas that might smooth your path:

• Consider writing out what you want to say in advance. Your general style may be to go into a meeting with your adviser without having a clear sense of why you're there. I suggest to all my clients that they set a clear purpose for every meeting they have related to the dissertation. An intention is both a statement and a goal, something like, "I intend to meet with Dr. Brown and to feel empowered in my ideas. I want to leave the meeting with a clear deadline and a sense of being supported by him." Now, by taking the time to set an intention before the meeting, you have defined what you're doing there and what you want from the meeting. Taking this approach can give you a sense of focus, calm, and empowerment in what might otherwise be stressful situation. ABD clients who have used this approach have reported a significant improvement in how they feel in dealing with their advisers, and a significant improvement in the quality and output of these meetings. Keep in mind that this intention is by and about you; it's a statement of how you want to feel and what you want to accomplish. You can't set intentions for anyone else.

• Posture works wonders. I learned this from Tony Robbins, a world-famous self-development guru. In one of his programs, Tony explains that the majority of our feelings are somehow related to our body posture and how we carry ourselves during stressful situations. Tony recommends that we sit with our shoulders back, chin up, and hold this posture during every stressful event. I used this recently with a group coaching client who was slated to speak with her adviser the next day. During the group, I asked her to pay attention to her posture and to keep lifting her chin and squaring off her shoulders as she practiced what she wanted to say. As a result, she felt more confident during the practice session, and she used this technique through the course of the call, with extremely positive results. In her own words, "posture works wonders." I have used this myself whenever I was being given some negative news such as not being selected for a nationally syndicated advice column. By taking the bad news with my shoulders back and chin up, I think I got over the rejection much more quickly.

• Clarify all requests. Often, advisers will suggest more books to read, articles to obtain, and topics to consider. Too often, ABDs take all this in without asking for clarification. A good question to ask is: "Is this something that's necessary to my project now?" This question can save you endless hours of frustration researching and writing and then taking it all out anyway. This clarification process is especially critical for those of you who have advisers who are big picture thinkers or who have lots of ideas. Rather than taking all the ideas in and getting overwhelmed and stuck, practice clarifying which ideas must be done right now and which can wait until later. If you ask this politely and with respect, your adviser is not likely to mind. Be sure to clarify when you don't understand the scope of any request or suggestion-this can save you endless hours of strain, worry, and frustration.

• Take good care of yourself. If meeting with your adviser is always stressful, you want to make doubly certain that you're taking good care of yourself after meeting or speaking with him/her. Take yourself out for lunch or a walk, watch a favorite show, do anything you can do to distract yourself and get started on the road to feeling better again.

Remember, you will always work more productively if you aim to feel better first and then work, rather than feeling bad and then trying to force yourself to work anyway. Feel better first, and your work will proceed much more smoothly.

Asking for What You Want: a model:

For those of you who could use a bit more practice or ideas for ways to speak with your advisers, here are some additional tips:

Take the time to get really clear on what you're asking for. This may mean making a list, or writing in your journal, or otherwise figuring out what you really want. Knowing what you want will make it easier to ask for-and to respond appropriately if alternatives are offered.

Practice stating your request clearly. Once you're clear on what you're asking for, it is often a good idea to practice out loud. Where possible, keep it simple and to the point, cutting out unnecessary words or phrases. This step can help you build confidence.

As you go into the place of stating your request (the meeting with your adviser or writing group), take a minute and run through, mentally, how you want the conversation to proceed. Taking a few seconds to fast-forward and visualize your desired outcome increases the likelihood of it occurring. See and feel your desired outcome as fully as possible.

After making your request, leave space for the other person to respond. Very often, after asking for something (especially if we're on edge or uncertain), we tend to fill in the space with nervous laughter or conversation. This decreases the impact of our request. Try reminding yourself to state your request and then pause, allowing the other person time to process and respond. It's common to feel nervous when asking for something. Do what you can to keep this from overwhelming the power of your request.

If the answer is not what you've hoped for, take a moment to check in with yourself before responding. Taking this time will allow you to take the next right steps-to withdraw, ask again, or offer a modified request.

Just remember, however the situation unfolds, you always have a better chance of getting what you want when you make the effort to ask.

Difficulties Dealing With Rejection

Rejection is always difficult, no matter what. I am not sure it ever gets easier to take, though I think we can all be more resilient than we are and therefore get over the rejection much more quickly.

In my forthcoming book *From Rejection to Success- the SMART way*, I outline a five-step model designed to assist individuals in becoming more rejection-resilient. I will share relevant aspects of my model below, and invite you to obtain the book should you desire more information.

The SMART model for dealing with rejection:

S: Self Care. Take the time to make yourself feel better. Get some exercise, treat yourself to a massage, or eat a scoop of your favorite ice cream. Pet your cat, call a friend, watch a comedy.

M: Meaning. Start to find another meaning for events. Often, we look at the whole world through one particular lens, a filter that is clouded by our own opinions, assumptions, and fears. We tend to ascribe meaning to all events based on our own fears. Instead, I encourage you to find another meaning, preferably one that is completely and totally opposite of what you would normally assume. Meaning is self-generated, so why not choose one that makes you feel good?

Let me give you an example: One of my clients, Nan*, submitted an abstract to a respected journal in her field. The abstract was rejected. Nan usually assumed that rejection meant she was not good enough. Instead, when she tried to find a completely opposite meaning (with my help), we came up with the meaning that the journal wasn't ready for the brilliance of Nan's abstract. Now, you might be shaking your head and thinking, "That's probably not true." Instead, what I suggest is that the meaning you make is only designed to help you feel better so you can start moving again. We ascribe meanings all the time, and not all of them are true. Why not, then, think something that makes you feel better instead of something that doesn't?

Another issue related to finding a new meaning is that you want to find a way to view the situation so that you don't take it as a personal attack. For Nan, she needed to find a meaning that made it about her work, not about her as a person. Then, for good measure, she needed to find a completely opposite meaning, shifting the rejection from being about her "lack" to being about her "brilliance." What you're looking to do here is find a way to flip the situation so you look at it in a new way that, hopefully, will make you laugh or at least giggle. That's when you know you've found a new meaning.

Start small. If you can't make a complete 180-degree flip from feeling bad to feeling good, try baby-stepping your way there. Maybe you'll start out thinking, "Other people liked this abstract" and you'll stay at that place for a while. Then, maybe the next day, you say, "I really liked this abstract" and you stay there for a while. Then, maybe on the third day, you say, "Wow, this abstract is great! They just couldn't see it." And on the fourth, "I'm brilliant, and they weren't ready for it." It's okay to find meaning in small

*Name has been changed.

bits. Aim for ideas you can believe right now and then keep shifting them closer and closer to something even more positive.

One of the best things you can ever learn to do is find another meaning for your failures and appreciate yourself for your successes. Once you find a new meaning, then you're ready for the next step:

A: Analyze & Appreciate. This is a difficult step, but the next piece of the model is to find something, no matter how small, to appreciate in this situation. It might be that the rejection was quick, or that you didn't feel as bad as the previous time this happened, or that it's a nice day outside. You just want to start shifting your attitude from one of "What's wrong with me?" to one where you are finding something to appreciate about who and where you are in this moment. The more you do this, the easier it gets to do. You also want to analyze the possible reasons for the rejection. Did the journal recently change focus and you didn't know? Are there some clues or cues you can use to approach this differently next time?

R: Readiness. This is a stage of preparation, where you take your new meaning, mix it in with your analysis and appreciation, and then find some new actions to take that will move you closer to your goal. Hint: eating bonbons in your pajamas for days and days will not get your dissertation written. So, this step, readiness, is about preparing whatever you need to get back in the game and try again.

T: Try again. This is the step where you actually get back to work, revising the manuscript, editing the manuscript, doing more research, going back to talk to your adviser again, whatever. The most important aspect of trying again is taking some action that moves you closer to what you want.

Just Do One Thing

In my practice, this principle is called "Just do one thing." It doesn't matter what that action is or how small it is; once you have taken an action in the direction of what you want, you have gently committed yourself to that path. When I began writing this book, I didn't think of it as "I need to write about 140 pages in a month", though that was what I ended up doing. Instead, I tried to stay focused on just doing one thing each day to bring this book closer to being created. Most days, this "one thing" was writing; sometimes for an hour, sometimes for just ten minutes. On other days, the "one thing" was finding an editor or book design person. Another time, it was deciding on marketing and promotion for this book. Other times, it was sitting outside for a few minutes and contemplating the next topics to include. The most important thing, though, was that every day, I was working on the book or working on aspects related to this book. By staying focused on doing one thing, I was able to accomplish a great deal in a very short amount of time. A similar approach has aided many of my clients in making progress on their dissertations, especially when they were feeling overwhelmed or stuck due to interpersonal conflict and other similar issues.

So far, I've never met anyone who moved through the dissertation process without experiencing at least one rejection. While rejection never feels good, there are certain strategies that can make it easier to manage.

If you are currently experiencing a rejection and you're finding it difficult to get back to work, try these strategies to overcome the negative feelings and get back to work on the dissertation. Here are some additional ideas to assist you:

•Allow yourself to experience your feelings. This may mean anger, sadness, irritation, annoyance, anything related to what has occurred. The sooner you allow your feelings to come out, the sooner you can get them out of your way.

• Revisit your past successes. When something doesn't go as planned, there is often a tendency for us to forget all the times when our life did go exactly (or better!) than we planned. If you have been keeping a success journal, as I previously suggested, please do refer to it when you need a reminder of how accomplished and capable you really are.

• Don't take it personally. I know, I know, we've all heard this one before. I'm not sure, all the time, that I understand how not to take it personally, but here are some ideas I have. Perhaps we can think of the rejection as a "no, not now" rather than a "no, not ever." Knowing that we will likely have another chance or opportunity to go after what we want may take some of the sting out of not getting it this time.

• Look for the positive aspects of the situation. Again, this can be challenging to do, but is definitely worth it. No matter how unfair, or negative, or otherwise "not good" something is, there is probably something positive in it, somewhere. If nothing else, we've learned more about what we absolutely, positively do not want. That gives us clarity and can help in future actions.

• Develop support in many different areas of your life. The best time to create new support is when you are happy and feeling great. Having some extra support structures-whether making a few new acquaintances or strengthening ties with longtime friends-can go a long way in softening any of the rejections of life. Take a few minutes to deposit some extra kindnesses in the "bank" of your relationships; you'll have a lot more to withdraw whenever you need it.

Remember, rejection is but a moment-and it can be over as soon as you're ready to let it go.

Lack of Mentor/Collegial Relationships

Another factor impacting dissertation progress is related to a lack of mentoring/collegial relationships. This is not exactly the same as having unresolved conflicts with your adviser. In that situation, you are somewhat involved with your adviser, and s/he comments on and criticizes your work. When you lack a mentor/collegial relationship, you might not have an adviser with whom to work, or you might be between advisers, or you might have an adviser who seems "too busy" to work with you and who comes across as distant, uncaring, or cold.

If you are without a strong support system, you will want to take several actions to help you bridge this gap. Similar to the suggestions made earlier in the book, you want to create a strong support system in both the academic and personal realms to make up for what you might be missing within your department. While it may not be fair that you have to seek this support outside of your school-especially when you pay tuition and support the school-life is not fair. Would you rather worry about fairness or would you finish? Let's presume you can't do both. Which will it be?

If you have decided your answer is finishing, and I sincerely hope it is, then you need to take action now to meet your needs. If you don't meet your needs, no one else is likely to step up to do it for you.

If you are experiencing a lack of mentoring/collegiality in your dissertation process, here are some steps you can take:

•Seek out online support. Do a search for virtual dissertation support groups and check out Web sites relating to dissertating and the dissertation process.

•Seek out practical support. Making contacts with people who can assist you with typing, data entry, statistics, and so forth can be a strong start to developing the collegiality you desire.

•Start an in-person dissertation support group. All you need for this is a small flier at the local coffee shop or ad in the community newspaper or even a note through the school's e-mail list. The text might read something like:
Seeking fellow ABDs in all fields who would like to meet once a (week or month) for dissertation support. Friendly atmosphere, size limited. Contact (your name/e-mail/phone) for more information.

•Make contact with those who recently completed your program. See if any of them would be willing to act as an informal mentor. This can be especially helpful if this person worked with some of the same faculty members with whom you will be involved.

•Be supportable. When you reach out to people, be sure to allow them to help you. I once worked with a woman who wanted coaching, but then proceeded to negate every suggestion I made. After a while, it became clear that she was finding it difficult to allow herself to be supported; she equated getting support with being weak. If you reach out to others, allow them to assist you.

•Be supportive. If you can mentor or assist others, consider doing so, even in a limited way. I believe what you put out into the world comes back to you, so if you want a mentor and colleagues, be a good mentor and colleague.

•Be an active participant in this process. You will not usually meet a lot of colleagues or mentors if you spend every day shuffling back and forth from the kitchen to the computer wearing your pajamas. If you want to meet new people, make it a goal to be actively out there seeking these people. Join local book clubs, departmental conferences, meetings, anywhere you are likely to find people who are like you. Make the first overture of friendship-invite someone out for coffee.

Personal Relationship Problems

Personal relationship problems are another significant factor impacting your capacity to make progress on the dissertation. These relationship problems may be of the romantic variety (such as with a spouse, partner, or significant other) or they can be familial (ailing family member, difficulties in your family of origin), social (problems dealing with friends or room-mates) or career related (downsizing, job loss, job change). Whatever the source, personal problems can take a toll on your energy and motivation and can sap your dissertation time.

If you are currently experiencing significant personal relationship stress, you may need to take a break from the dissertation process to resolve this situation. If you are caring for an ailing family member or going through a divorce, you'll need to balance out your responsibilities and tasks while determining how much you can realistically work on the dissertation. If, however, you decide that finishing the dissertation remains one of your top three goals (after self care and caring for your family member/relative), then you may want to keep in mind the following tips to maximize your dissertation progress:

•Get used to working in small bits of time. Even ten minutes of time, applied regularly, can add up to significant progress. Get in the habit of working on your dissertation first thing in the morning. Read a few pages of an article, take a few notes, write a few lines, anything that signifies progress on this task. There is a common misconception that you can only produce quality work after spending thirty hours a day on your dissertation. This is simply not true. Do at least one ten-minute chunk of work on your dissertation at least five days per week, and you'll be surprised at the progress you can make in small chunks. If you are taking care of a baby or relative, try to grab a few minutes of time early in the morning, and then rest during the day if needed. It's more effective to work on the dissertation first thing, because, like exercising, it's tough to get back to it once you've put it off until the afternoon or evening.

•Keep a running to-do list. This is a good technique no matter what. But it's especially helpful when you're thinking about ideas and what to do next, but can't actually get to work on it for a few hours (or a day or two). Keep track of your ideas and thoughts, maybe in a dissertation journal, and you'll have your brilliance recorded for future use.

•Lower your expectations. When you are juggling multiple responsibilities, you want to keep your expectations reasonable. You are, in fact, only human. Believe it or not.

•Reward yourself for what you do accomplish. When moving through an emotionally difficult time, it's common for each of us to shift into "survival/scarcity" mode, where we deprive ourselves of experiences that would support and nurture us. Rather than shrinking your life and contracting it around work, work, and more work, do what you can to take care of yourself along the way. Get some help with your project or with caretaking, take an afternoon nap occasionally, spend a bit of time in meditation or prayer if you find this helpful, in essence, find ways to build your resilience as you move toward your goals.

Building resilience can be achieved by using this fairly simple model that came out of some recent coaching work with my individual and group clients.

I had been noticing that many of my clients were working on themes related to building resilience. They were practicing new ways of thinking and acting that had helped them to be more successful at meeting the demands of their lives.

Since I believe that whatever is showing up in my coaching

sessions is a microcosm of what the larger community is experiencing, I thought it might be helpful to focus on strategies for building resilience.

Most stress comes from hitting a point where the input coming in is more than we can take. Our threshold has been surpassed and we go into a state of being over-whelmed. For some people, that becomes a way of life. These are the same people who experience a greater frequency of medical, relational, financial and other problems in their lives.

Luckily, there is a pretty simple technique for immediately reducing stress. It's called taking a break. A break is defined as any activity that rejuvenates or refreshes you. If you start interspersing periods of intense work with short breaks, you will gradually raise your stress threshold. In raising your stress threshold, you will find yourself being able to achieve much more without getting overwhelmed.

Similar to weight lifting, in which you work a muscle to fatigue and then rest it, I believe we can do a similar kind of training for our lives. If you are ready to build your resilience, you can get started by looking over your appointment book or schedule and starting to build in about three to five ten- to fifteen-minute rest periods per day. Try to schedule these breaks between tasks.

I find that the simple act of taking a ten-minute break a few times a day has improved my productivity and my outlook. I'm better able to step away from problems and come up with creative solutions, and I have noticed an increase in my capacity to tolerate uncertainty.

Learn to find joy in as many moments as possible. This will increase your resilience. The greater your threshold for the uncertainties of life, the better able you'll be to excel with ease.

The dissertation is not really a test of your intelligence or capability. Instead, it is a means to strengthen and build upon your capacities for patience, perseverance, and diligence. This is a crucial distinction, because it's not about "Can you do this?" It's really about "How can you do this?"

As we come to the end of this book, I trust and hope that you feel more confident about yourself and your ability to complete this project successfully in a reasonable time frame. Once all the pieces click into place, it is quite common for dissertators to complete their dissertations in a year or less. In fact, I've coached a great many students to do just that.

If you are serious about obtaining your Ph.D., remember several ideas in particular:

1) Suffering is not good.
2) Keep your life as simple as possible.
3) Take care of you.
4) Reward yourself along the way.
5) Show up to the dissertation work at least five days per week.
6) Ask for help.
7) Accept help when it shows up.
8) Stay connected to important people.
9) Remember what this is for.
10) Recognize that you're always doing the best you can.

If any day doesn't go quite as planned, leave that day behind you and start over as soon as possible. Let go of any past failures or mistakes and welcome the present. Every day brings you more opportunities to complete this project. Take every opportunity you can to complete this once and for all.

Remember, the process is simple, but not easy. Thousands

of people have already done it, and so can you.

In closing, I'd like to leave you with the words of a very wise Irish proverb that I believe sums up the dissertation process quite well:

> *When things go wrong as they sometimes will.*
> *When the road you're trudging seems all up hill.*
> *When funds are low and the debts are high.*
> *And you want to smile, but you have to sigh.*
> *When care is pressing you down a bit.*
> *Rest, if you must, but don't you quit.*
> *Life is queer with its twists and turns.*
> *As everyone of us sometimes learns.*
> *And many a failure turns about.*
> *When he might have won had he stuck it out:*
> *Don't give up though the pace seems slow -*
> *You may succeed with another blow.*
> *Success is failure turned inside out -*
> *The silver tint of the clouds of doubt*
> *And you never can tell how close you are.*
> *It may be near when it seems so far:*
> *So stick to the fight when you're hardest hit -*
> *It's when things seem worst that you must not quit.*
> *- Author unknown*

You can do this. I know it. Rest if you must, but don't you quit!
Wishing you excellence and ease on your dissertation journey,
Rachna

About
the author

Dr. Rachna D. Jain is a licensed psychologist and professional coach who developed the "Get it Done!" (sm) coaching process to aid dissertation writers to complete their projects in a year or less.

Rachna is in a unique position to assist dissertation writers, as she has written two books of coaching strategies for dissertation completion *(Get it Done! A Coach's Guide to Dissertation Success, and Get it Done Faster: Secrets of Dissertation Success)*, and she has served for several years as Editor of the *All But Dissertation Survival Guide*, a twice-monthly e-mail newsletter focused on helping students complete their doctoral dissertations. Rachna's books have been adopted as required readings for several doctoral programs that offer courses on dissertation writing.

Rachna is a national expert on coaching, having been quoted in publications such as *The Washington Post, The Chicago Tribune, Fortune Small Business, Entrepreneur Magazine, Ladies' Home Journal, Self, Redbook, Shape, Cosmopolitan,First for Women and GradPsych*. In addition, she is a contributing editor to *Seventeen*.

A prolific writer and skilled speaker, Rachna offers workshops and seminars on successfully completing the Ph.D. She offers coaching groups for those looking to maximize their progress and get the *!*(&* dissertation done once and for all.

Based in Maryland, she can be reached online at http://www.CompleteYourDissertation.com

What People Say About the "Get it Done" (sm) Coaching Process:

"But thank you Rachna, I very clearly remember our tele-class, and how incredibly supportive you were, and how underlying it all there was always a sense that we must be tender and kind to ourselves, that we must support our-selves, and reward ourselves for hard work, and be gentle, always gentle -that got me through, it really did!! You had an ENORMOUS influence on my ability to finish, and now I preach that line to every ABD I meet! "Thank you!"
 -Linda (aka Dr. Linda Derksen, finally)

"Thanks for writing *Get it Done*! I found the book to be extremely helpful in moving me from dissertation despera-tion to hope in actually completing this project. The tips you offer are all timely and relevant.... I expect the book to be quite tattered by the time I'm finished.... In a small pack-age, you have made a huge difference in my work! Thank you!"
-David York, ABD, University of Missouri
(David has since completed his Ph.D.!)

"You were absolutely terrific in all aspects. Coaching was very helpful to me because I lacked self confidence. I fin-ished my dissertation in just about 18 months, and now I have landed a full-time teaching position for the Fall. Needless to say, I'm thrilled."
-Stephen Wagner, Ph.D.

"My experience with Dr. Rachna Jain as my dissertation

146

coach was FANTASTIC!! Coaching with Rachna allowed me to graduate quickly, and begin earning a better salary. Her coaching fee was well worth it!! I chose coaching because I was concerned about how full time employment, family obligations, moving away from my university, and isolation from my department could slow down my dissertation progress. During my time with Rachna, my department program was axed by the dean, and my chair lost her tenure. I was blessed to have Rachna as a coach and I finished in spite of all the department adversity! I've recommended Dr. Rachna Jain to all my friends and colleagues!"
-Neera Puri, Ph.D.

"I was floundering in my eighth year of doctoral work with a flimsy topic and no real proposal. Having completed my classwork, I felt alone and abandoned by the university and was not making any real progress. As a father of two working full time, there was always a reason not to work on my research. I knew, however, that I had to get serious to complete my dissertation within the mandated ten-year time frame, but did not know really where or how to start. Worse, I was beginning to doubt myself and my abilities to complete the research. It was then that I fortunately stumbled upon Excel with Ease Coaching.Com and Dr. Rachna Jain. In weekly coaching sessions, Dr. Jain put my seemingly insurmountable task in perspective. Within nine months of contacting Dr. Jain, my proposal was accepted, and my dissertation was unanimously approved without revision within ten months of my proposal review. Thank you, Dr. Jain, for showing me the way to reach my goal here.
-Bruce Myers, Ph.D.

"I got finished faster than I though I would and the process was more joyful than I ever thought it could be. I learned valuable tools to getting the dissertation done. I don't think I could have accomplished this feat without you."
-Ann Brewster, Ph.D.

Other recommended resources

Bolker, Joan. *Write Your Dissertation in Fifteen Minutes a Day*. New York: Henry Holt & Company, 1998.

Jain, Rachna. *Get it Done! A Coach's Guide to Dissertation Success*. Columbia, MD: MoonSwept Press, 2002.

Manning, Steve. http://www.writeabooknow.com

Perry, Susan. *Writing in Flow*. Cincinnati, OH: Writer's Digest Books, 1999.

Rasch, David. *Writing Productivity Problems*, 1997. http://www.dc.peachnet.edu/~shale/humanities/composition/handouts/selftalk.html

Rudestam, Kjell Erik and Newton, Rae R. *Surviving Your Dissertation: A Comprehensive Guide to Content and Process*. New York: Sage Publications, 2001.

All But Dissertation Survival Guide - a free email newsletter devoted to helping graduate students complete their dissertations. http://www.absurvivalguide.org

Phinished- an online forum for those seeking support and assistance regarding the dissertation process. http://www.phinished.org/

Endnote Bibliographic Software. http://www.endnote.com
Procite Bibliographic Software. http://www.procite.com

Get it Done Faster!

A special note about dissertation coaching:
One of the most significant decisions you can make regarding your dissertation process is that of choosing to hire a dissertation coach. Hiring a dissertation coach can result in a significant decrease in the length of time it takes to complete your dissertation. One of my former clients, for example, wrote her entire dissertation (six full chapters) in an eight month time span. She credits the structure and support provided by the coaching framework as a major factor in her very quick completion of her dissertation. If you are stuck in the dissertation process, or haven't been making significant progress over the past few months, you might want to consider working with a coach to get yourself back on track and moving forward. In an effort to assist you, I've provided some information (below) to address the most common questions graduate students have about working with a coach.

What is Coaching?

Coaching is a professional relationship between two people, the Coach and the Client. The Coach is there to completely support the Client so that the Client may reach his/her goals faster and easier.

The Coach supports the Client to strategize and implement behaviors which move the Client closer his/her goals.

What is Dissertation Coaching?

Dissertation coaching is a particular kind of coaching. The approach is the same as in general coaching, but the focus is more specialized directly on the dissertation. Most often, dissertation coaches help their clients set workable goals, implement good self care, and act as a "cheerleader".

Who sets the agenda for the Coaching?

The Client sets the agenda for each coaching session, and the Coach is there to ask questions, offer tips or hints, all in the framework of helping the Client get clear on what he/she wants to do. The Coach helps the Clients set reasonable goals and build forward momentum. The Coach will often guide the Client into finding new methods for accomplishing the dissertation work faster and more easily. The Client always has the final say and responsibility for his/her success.

How is Coaching Different From Psychotherapy Or Consulting?

Coaching is different from psychotherapy because the coaching relationship is one of equals- and is "co-created". In psychotherapy, the therapist is considered to be the "expert" and is expected to take a greater responsibility for the process and outcome of the relationship. Coaching is different from consulting, because the Coach helps the Client find the answers, where a consultant often recommends a certain approach or strategy.

Done well, coaching is like a "dance" between the Coach and Client- moving back and forth, weaving in and out, with the end result being greater forward movement for the Client.

How does Dissertation Coaching create change?

Dissertation coaching helps graduate students find new ways to tackle the "same old" problems. Using a combination of powerful questions, requests, and observations, the Coach helps move the Client into action.

What is the Structure of Dissertation Coaching?

The coaching format varies by the individual Coach. Most often, coaching sessions are held between two and four times per month, either by phone or face to face. Sessions may last from 30-45 minutes. The Client is requested to bring his/her successes, challenges, and questions to the coaching session. The Coach then helps the Client celebrate the successes and work through the challenges.

Can I get Good Results from Telephone Coaching?

Yes! It might take a bit of getting used to, but there is no difference in the level of success between virtual (telephone) coaching, and face to face coaching. And virtual coaching is much easier- just pick up the phone and dial. You can take part in the call from the privacy and comfort of your home or office.

Can I get coaching for just parts of the dissertation process?

Generally, coaching is contracted for on a month-by-month basis, so it is possible to work with a coach for a few months and then stop. I have found that my clients benefit most from at least three months of consecutive coaching. Most of my current clients have been with me for 6-9 months.

What is the Cost Of Dissertation Coaching?

This varies by professional, however, most coaches charge between $200-$500 per month for individual dissertation coaching, based on the structure and format. While this may seem expensive, you, very often, can take months (if not years) off your dissertation process by working with a Coach. The Coach may offer extras- such as editing, reading, etc., for an additional charge. Payment is collected in advance, at the beginning of a new month.

If sessions are held over the telephone, most often the Client is expected to absorb the cost of any long-distance calls.

Coaching is generally agreed to on a month-by-month basis, so it is possible to "try out" coaching for a month to see if it works for you. Most people obtain the greatest benefit from coaching when they commit to at least three consecutive months.

Should A Coach be an expert in my topic area?

This is not necessary. A Coach is there to help the Client through the process of completing the dissertation, therefore it is not necessary for the Coach to be an expert in the topic area. That is left to the Client.

Are reading and editing included in coaching?

Again, this depends on the particular Coach, and can be discussed in the initial session.

How can I know if coaching is the right option for me?

Many coaches offer a free initial consultation, which provides an opportunity to ask questions, and to ascertain level of "fit" between you and the Coach.

What questions should I ask a potential Coach?

Like in any other professional relationship, you might want to ask the Coach about his/her level of training and experience in coaching. As with any professional relationship, you would want to make sure that you're comfortable with the Coach's training, experience and background in this area.

While there are currently no standards or guidelines for who may use the designation, "Coach", you might want to find out whether the potential Coach has acquired formal coach training, or is in the process of acquiring this training. You may also want to ask how many Clients the Coach has worked with, and, also, ascertain how the Coach has helped Clients.

Is it possible to obtain references on a potential Coach?

This is at the discretion of the potential Coach. Some coaches will provide these, some won't- due to privacy, confidentiality, or other similar issues. Use your own best judgment and decide how important recommendations or references are in your mind.

Are there other benefits to Dissertation Coaching?

Yes! Students who work with coaches tend to complete their dissertations more quickly than those who don't.

Also, the skills, approaches, and strategies you acquire through dissertation coaching can be easily generalized to the rest of your life.

Coaching can help you find a better, easier way to reach your goals- and who couldn't benefit from that?

••If you'd like to learn more about the coaching options I offer, please visit
http://www.CompleteYourDissertation.com/blog
to get the most up to date listings and offerings.

Ordering Information

Please return this form to: Moonswept Press, 20203 Goshen Road #374, Gaithersburg, MD 20879
Orders must be accompanied by payment via check or money order or may be charged to MasterCard/Visa.
Orders may be faxed to 240-396-5773
Order online http://CompleteYourDissertation.com/go/books

To make inquiries, please email
info@completeyourdissertation.com

Please send me (indicate quantity)
____ Get It Done! $19.95
____ Postage and Handling ($6.00 per copy, US First Class Mail)
____ Maryland add 5% sales tax

____ Total Amount Due

☐ Check or Money Order enclosed, made payable to Rachna Jain
☐ Visa ☐ MasterCard

Name _____

Address _____

City _____ State _____ Zip _____

Daytime Phone _____

Email _____

Credit Card # _____

Exp. Date _____

Signature _____